College Accounting

EIGHTEENTH EDITION

James A. Heintz, DBA, CPA

Professor of Accounting, University of Kansas

Lawrence, Kansas

Robert W. Parry, Jr., PhD

Professor of Accounting, Indiana University

Bloomington, Indiana

Prepared by

Linda and William C. K. Alberts
National Business College

THOMSON

SOUTH-WESTERN

Australia · Canada · Mexico · Singapore · Spain · United Kingdom · United States

THOMSON

SOUTH-WESTERN

Instructor's Resource Guide for College Accounting, 18e, Chapters 1-16
By James A. Heintz and Robert W. Parry

Prepared by Linda and William C. K. Alberts

Vice President/Editorial Director
Jack Calhoun

Vice President/Editor-in-Chief
George Werthman

Publisher
Rob Dewey

Acquisitions Editor
Jennifer Codner

Sr. Developmental Editor
Sara Wilson

Sr. Marketing Manager
Larry Qualls

Marketing Channel Manager
Brian Joyner

Sr. Production Editor
Tim Bailey

Sr. Technology Project Editor
Sally Nieman

Sr. Media Editor
Robin K. Browning

Editorial Assistant
Janice Hughes

Sr. Design Project Manager
Michelle Kunkler

Manufacturing Coordinator
Doug Wilke

Cover Design
Lisa Albonetti,
Cincinnati, OH

Cover Images
© PhotoDisc, Inc.

Printer
Globus Printing

Table Of Contents

Chapter   **Page**

CORRELATION CHART, CHAPTERS 1-16

The following chart depicts how the number of the exercise or problem appeared in the last edition (17e) and how the corresponding item now appears in the new edition (18e).

	Number 17e	Number 18e		Number 17e	Number 18e
Chapter 1			**Chapter 2**		
Exercise	1-1A	1-1A	Exercise	2-7B	2-7B
	1-2A	1-2A	Problem	2-1B	2-8B
Exercise	1-1B	1-1B		2-2B	2-9B
	1-2B	1-2B		2-3B	2-10B
Chapter 2				2-4B	2-11B
Exercise	2-1A	2-1A		2-5B	2-12B
	2-2A	2-2A	Mastery Problem	1-5	No change
	2-3A	2-3A	Challenge Problem	—	No change
	2-4A	2-4A	**Chapter 3**		
	2-5A	2-5A	Exercise	3-1A	3-1A
	2-6A	2-6A		3-2A	3-2A
	2-7A	2-7A		3-3A	3-3A
Problem	2-1A	2-8A		3-4A	3-4A
	2-2A	2-9A		3-5A	3-5A
	2-3A	2-10A		3-6A	3-6A
	2-4A	2-11A		3-7A	3-7A
	2-5A	2-12A		3-8A	3-8A
Exercise	2-1B	2-1B		3-9A	3-9A
	2-2B	2-2B		3-10A	3-10A
	2-3B	2-3B		3-11A	3-11A
	2-4B	2-4B		3-12A	3-12A
	2-5B	2-5B	Problem	3-1A	3-13A
	2-6B	2-6B		3-2A	3-14A

	Number 17e	Number 18e		Number 17e	Number 18e
Chapter 3			**Chapter 4**		
Problem	3-3A	3-15A	Exercise	4-8A	4-8A
Exercise	3-1B	3-1B	Problem	4-1A	4-9A
	3-2B	3-2B		4-2A	4-10A
	3-3B	3-3B		4-3A	4-11A
	3-4B	3-4B	Exercise	4-1B	4-1B
	3-5B	3-5B		4-2B	4-2B
	3-6B	3-6B		4-3B	4-3B
	3-7B	3-7B		4-4B	4-4B
	3-8B	3-8B		4-5B	4-5B
	3-9B	3-9B		4-6B	4-6B
	3-10B	3-10B		4-7B	4-7B
	3-11B	3-11B		4-8B	4-8B
	3-12B	3-12B	Problem	4-1B	4-9B
Problem	3-1B	3-13B		4-2B	4-10B
	3-2B	3-14B		4-3B	4-11B
	3-3B	3-15B	Mastery Problem	1-2	No change
Mastery Problem	1-6	No change	Challenge Problem	—	No change
Challenge Problem	1-2	No change	**Chapter 5**		
Chapter 4			Exercise	5-1A	5-1A
Exercise	4-1A	4-1A		5-2A	5-2A
	4-2A	4-2A		5-3A	5-3A
	4-3A	4-3A		5-4A	5-4A
	4-4A	4-4A		5-5A	5-5A
	4-5A	4-5A		5-6A	5-6A
	4-6A	4-6A		5-7A	5-7A
	4-7A	4-7A		5-8A	5-8A

	Number 17e	Number 18e		Number 17e	Number 18e
Chapter 5			**Chapter 5**		
Exercise	5-9A	5-9A	Challenge Problem	1-2	No change
	5-10A	5-10A	Exercise	5Apx-1A	5Apx-1A
	5-11A	5-11A		5Apx-2A	5Apx-2A
	5-12A	5-12A		5Apx-3A	5Apx-3A
Problem	5-1A	5-13A		5Apx-4A	5Apx-4A
	5-2A	5-14A		5Apx-1B	5Apx-1B
	5-3A	5-15A		5Apx-2B	5Apx-2B
	5-4A	5-16A		5Apx-3B	5Apx-3B
Exercise	5-1B	5-1B		5Apx-4B	5Apx-4B
	5-2B	5-2B	**Chapter 6**		
	5-3B	5-3B	Exercise	6-1A	6-1A
	5-4B	5-4B		6-2A	6-2A
	5-5B	5-5B		6-3A	6-3A
	5-6B	5-6B		6-4A	6-4A
	5-7B	5-7B		6-5A	6-5A
	5-8B	5-8B	Problem	6-1A	6-6A
	5-9B	5-9B		6-2A	6-7A
	5-10B	5-10B		6-3A	6-8A
	5-11B	5-11B	Exercise	6-1B	6-1B
	5-12B	5-12B		6-2B	6-2B
Problem	5-1B	5-13B		6-3B	6-3B
	5-2B	5-14B		6-4B	6-4B
	5-3B	5-15B		6-5B	6-5B
	5-4B	5-16B	Problem	6-1B	6-6B
Mastery Problem	1-2	No change		6-2B	6-7B

	Number 17e	Number 18e		Number 17e	Number 18e
Chapter 6			**Chapter 7**		
Problem	6-3B	6-8B	Exercise	7-6B	7-6B
Mastery Problem	—	No change		7-7B	7-7B
Challenge Problem	—	No change		7-8B	7-8B
Exercise	6Apx-1A	6Apx-1A		7-9B	7-9B
Problem	6Apx-1A	6Apx-2A	Problem	7-1B	7-10B
Exercise	6Apx-1B	6Apx-1B		7-2B	7-11B
Problem	6Apx-1B	6Apx-2B	Mastery Problem	1-3	No change
Comp. Prob. 1 (Pt. 1)	1-11	No change	Challenge Problem	1-2	No change
Comp. Prob. 1 (Pt. 2)	N/A	New	**Chapter 8**		
Chapter 7			Exercise	8-1A	8-1A
Exercise	7-1A	7-1A		8-2A	8-2A
	7-2A	7-2A		8-3A	8-3A
	7-3A	7-3A		8-4A	8-4A
	7-4A	7-4A		8-5A	8-5A
	7-5A	7-5A		8-6A	8-6A
	7-6A	7-6A		8-7A	8-7A
	7-7A	7-7A	Problem	8-1A	8-8A
	7-8A	7-8A		8-2A	8-9A
	7-9A	7-9A		8-3A	8-10A
Problem	7-1A	7-10A	Exercise	8-1B	8-1B
	7-2A	7-11A		8-2B	8-2B
Exercise	7-1B	7-1B		8-3B	8-3B
	7-2B	7-2B		8-4B	8-4B
	7-3B	7-3B		8-5B	8-5B
	7-4B	7-4B		8-6B	8-6B
	7-5B	7-5B		8-7B	8-7B

	Number 17e	Number 18e		Number 17e	Number 18e
Chapter 8			**Chapter 10**		
Problem	8-1B	8-8B	Exercise	10-1A	10-1A
	8-2B	8-9B		10-2A	10-2A
	8-3B	8-10B		10-3A	10-3A
Mastery Problem	1-3	No change	Problem	10-1A	10-4A
Challenge Problem	1-2	No change		10-2A	10-5A
Chapter 9			Exercise	10-1B	10-1B
Exercise	9-1A	9-1A		10-2B	10-2B
	9-2A	9-2A		10-3B	10-3B
	9-3A	9-3A	Problem	10-1B	10-4B
	9-4A	9-4A		10-2B	10-5B
	9-5A	9-5A	Mastery Problem	1-3	No change
	9-6A	9-6A	Challenge Problem	—	No change
Problem	9-1A	9-7A	**Chapter 11**		
	9-2A	9-8A	Exercise	11-1A	11-1A
	9-3A	9-9A		11-2A	11-2A
Exercise	9-1B	9-1B		11-3A	11-3A
	9-2B	9-2B		11-4A	11-4A
	9-3B	9-3B		11-5A	11-5A
	9-4B	9-4B		11-6A	11-6A
	9-5B	9-5B		11-7A	11-7A
	9-6B	9-6B	Problem	11-1A	11-8A
Problem	9-1B	9-7B		11-2A	11-9A
	9-2B	9-8B		11-3A	11-10A
	9-3B	9-9B	Exercise	11-1B	11-1B
Mastery Problem	—	No change		11-2B	11-2B
Challenge Problem	—	No change		11-3B	11-3B

	Number 17e	Number 18e		Number 17e	Number 18e
Chapter 11			**Chapter 12**		
Exercise	11-4B	11-4B	Exercise	12-4B	12-4B
	11-5B	11-5B		12-5B	12-5B
	11-6B	11-6B		12-6B	12-6B
	11-7B	11-7B		12-7B	12-7B
Problem	11-1B	11-8B		12-8B	12-8B
	11-2B	11-9B	Problem	12-1B	12-9B
	11-3B	11-10B		12-2B	12-10B
Mastery Problem	1-3	No change		12-3B	12-11B
Challenge Problem	—	No change		12-4B	12-12B
Chapter 12			Mastery Problem	1-4	No change
Exercise	12-1A	12-1A	Challenge Problem	—	No change
	12-2A	12-2A	Exercise	12Apx-1A	12Apx-1A
	12-3A	12-3A		12Apx-2A	12Apx-2A
	12-4A	12-4A		12Apx-1B	12Apx-1B
	12-5A	12-5A		12Apx-2B	12Apx-2B
	12-6A	12-6A	**Chapter 13**		
	12-7A	12-7A	Exercise	N/A	13-1A (New)
	12-8A	12-8A		13-1A	13-2A
Problem	12-1A	12-9A		13-2A	13-3A
	12-2A	12-10A		13-3A	13-4A
	12-3A	12-11A		13-4A	13-5A
	12-4A	12-12A	Problem	13-1A	13-6A
Exercise	12-1B	12-1B		13-2A	13-7A
	12-2B	12-2B		13-3A	13-8A
	12-3B	12-3B		13-4A	13-9A

	Number 17e	Number 18e		Number 17e	Number 18e
Chapter 13			**Chapter 14**		
Problem	13-5A	13-10A	Problem	14-1A	14-8A*
	13-6A	13-11A		14-2A	14-9A
	13-7A	13-12A		14-3A	14-10A
Exercise	N/A	13-1B (New)		14-4A	14-11A
	13-1B	13-2B	Exercise	14-1B	14-1B
	13-2B	13-3B		14-2B	14-2B
	13-3B	13-4B		14-3B	14-3B
	13-4B	13-5B		14-4B	14-4B
Problem	13-1B	13-6B		14-5B	14-5B
	13-2B	13-7B		14-6B	14-6B
	13-3B	13-8B		14-7B	14-7B
	13-4B	13-9B	Problem	14-1B	14-8B
	13-5B	13-10B		14-2B	14-9B
	13-6B	13-11B		14-3B	14-10B
	13-7B	13-12B		14-4B	14-11B
Mastery Problem	1-2	No change	Mastery Problem	1-3	No change
Challenge Problem	—	No change	Challenge Problem	—	No change
Chapter 14			**Chapter 15**		
Exercise	14-1A	14-1A	Exercise	15-1A	15-1A
	14-2A	14-2A		15-2A	15-2A
	14-3A	14-3A		15-3A	15-3A
	14-4A	14-4A		15-4A	15-4A
	14-5A	14-5A		15-5A	15-5A
	14-6A	14-6A		15-6A	15-6A
	14-7A	14-7A		N/A	15-7 (New)

*No. 3 from this problem in 17e has been deleted in 18e.

	Number 17e	Number 18e
Chapter 15		
Exercise	N/A	15-8 (New)
Problem	15-1A	15-9A
	15-2A	15-10A
	15-3A	15-11A
	15-4A	15-12A
Exercise	15-1B	15-1B
	15-2B	15-2B
	15-3B	15-3B
	15-4B	15-4B
	15-5B	15-5B
	15-6B	15-6B
	N/A	15-7 (New)
	N/A	15-8 (New)
Problem	15-1B	15-9B
	15-2B	15-10B
	15-3B	15-11B
	15-4B	15-12B
Mastery Problem	1-2	No change
Challenge Problem	—	No change
Exercise	15Apx-1A	15Apx-1A
	15Apx-1B	15Apx-1B
Chapter 16		
Exercise	16-1A	16-1A
	16-2A	16-2A
	16-3A	16-3A
	16-4A	16-4A

	Number 17e	Number 18e
Chapter 16		
Exercise	16-5A	16-5A
	16-6A	16-6A
	16-7A	16-7A
Problem	16-1A	16-8A
	16-2A	16-9A
	16-3A	16-10A
Exercise	16-1B	16-1B
	16-2B	16-2B
	16-3B	16-3B
	16-4B	16-4B
	16-5B	16-5B
	16-6B	16-6B
	16-7B	16-7B
Problem	16-1B	16-8B
	16-2B	16-9B
	16-3B	16-10B
Comp. Prob. 2:		
Gen. Journ., Pt. 1	N/A	New
Gen. Journ., Pt. 2	N/A	New
Spec. Journ., Pt. 1*	2–3	2–3
	3, 6, & 7	1, 2, 3, 6, 7 & 9
	4–9	4–9
Spec. Journ., Pt. 2*	2–3	2–3
	3, 6, & 7	1, 2, 3, 6, 7 & 9
	4–9	4–9

*In 18e, Parts 1 and 2 titles were changed from Accounting Cycle with Subsidiary Ledgers, Part 1 and Part 2 to Special Journals Based, Part 1 and 2.

Chapter 1
Introduction to Accounting

Learning Objectives

LO1   Describe the purpose of accounting.
LO2   Describe the accounting process.
LO3   Define GAAP and describe the process used to develop these principles.
LO4   Define three types of business ownership structures.
LO5   Classify different types of businesses by activities.
LO6   Identify career opportunities in accounting.

Teaching Tips

➢   Chapter 1 should be fairly easy for students to understand on their own. It is intended to provide background information on the purpose of accounting, the general process, types of ownership structures, business activities, and career opportunities. It can be covered in the first class session after attending to administrative matters.

➢   If you prefer to jump right into the accounting equation and the analysis of transactions, you can let the students read this chapter on their own and start with Chapter 2.

LO1

❖   **PowerPoint Slides 1-1 through 1-3 present The Purpose of Accounting**

I.   The Purpose of Accounting
    A.   Provides financial information about the financial condition of a business to individuals, agencies, and organizations.

❖   **Transparency Master 1-1 illustrates Figure 1-1 Users of Accounting Information**
❖   **PowerPoint Slide 1-4 presents the same information**

    B.   Users of accounting information **(See Figure 1-1)**
        1.   Owners
        2.   Managers
        3.   Creditors
        4.   Government agencies

In-Class Exercise: Complete Exercise 1-1A, 1-1B (10 minutes each)

LO2

❖ Transparency Master 1-2 illustrates Figure 1-2 The Accounting Process
❖ PowerPoint Slides 1-5 through 1-14 present the same information

II.   The Accounting Process **(See Figure 1-2)**

Teaching Tip

➢   Discussing the accounting process provides an opportunity to point out that the best way to learn accounting is by doing something. Yes, students must read the chapters. However, most learning takes place while answering questions, writing memos, and working the exercises and problems. Remind your students that it is very important to do the homework as it is assigned. They shouldn't wait until a few days before the examination to work the problems.

A.   **Accounting** is the art of gathering financial information about a business and reporting this information to users.

B.   The six major steps of the accounting process are as follows:
   1.   **Analyzing**
      a)   Looking at events that have taken place.
      b)   Thinking about how these events have affected the business.
   2.   **Recording**
      a)   Business transactions are entered into an accounting system.
      b)   Accounting systems can be done manually or by the use of computers.
   3.   **Classifying**
      a)   Sorting and grouping similar items together.
      b)   Business accounts are classified.
   4.   **Summarizing**
      a)   Bringing various items of information together.
      b)   Determines a result.
   5.   **Reporting**
      a)   Communicating results.
      b)   Results are communicated in the form of financial statements.
   6.   **Interpreting**
      a)   Deciding the importance of reported information.
      b)   Uses percentage analyses and ratios to explain how pieces of information relate to one another.

In-Class Exercise: Complete Exercise 1-2A, 1-2B (10 minutes each)

LO3

III.   Generally accepted accounting principles (GAAP)
   A.   Developed by Financial Accounting Standards Board (FASB).
   B.   Provides concepts and guidelines to be followed during the accounting process.

   C.   The five steps for adopting a standard.

1. Issue placed on agenda.
2. Discussion memorandum issued.
3. Public hearings held around country.
4. Issuance of exposure draft.
5. Final statement of financial accounting standards (SFAS) issued.

LO4

❖ **Transparency Master 1-3 illustrates Figure 1-3 Types of Ownership Structures**
❖ **PowerPoint Slides 1-15 through 1-18 present the same information**

III. Three Types of Ownership Structures (See **Figure 1-3**)
   A. **Sole Proprietorship**
      1. Business is owned by one person.
      2. Owner assumes all the risks for the business personally.
      3. Owner makes all of the business decisions.
   B. **Partnership**
      1. Business is owned by more than one person.
      2. Partners assume all the risks for the business personally.
      3. Owners share risks and decision making.
      4. Partners may disagree about the way the business should be run.
   C. **Corporation**
      1. Business is owned by stockholders.
      2. Owners' risks are limited to their initial investment.
      3. In publicly owned corporations, shareholders often have very little influence on business decisions.

Teaching Tip

➢ Most businesses in the United States operate as sole proprietorships or partnerships. However, corporations earn the highest amount of revenue. The largest corporations in the United States are known as the "Fortune 500."

LO5

❖ **Transparency Master 1-4 illustrates Figure 1-4 Types and Examples of Businesses**
❖ **PowerPoint Slides 1-19 through 1-22 present the same information**

IV. Types of Business **(See Figure 1-4)**
   A. **Service business** provides a service.
   B. **Merchandising business** buys a product from a business to sell at the retail level.
   C. **Manufacturing business** makes a product to sell.

LO6

❖ **Transparency Master 1-5 illustrates Figure 1-5 Accounting Careers**
❖ **PowerPoint Slides 1-23 through 1-31 present the same information**

V. Career Opportunities in Accounting (See **Figure 1-5**)
   A. **Accounting Clerks**
      1. Record, sort, and file accounting information.

2. Specialize in various areas of accounting.
3. Require at least one year of accounting education.

B. **Bookkeepers**
    1. Supervise the work of accounting clerks, perform daily accounting work, and summarize accounting information.
    2. Require one to two years of education and some experience.

C. **Para-accountants**
    1. Provide accounting, auditing, or tax services under the direct supervision of an accountant.
    2. Generally requires a two-year degree and significant experience.

D. **Accountants**
    1. Design the accounting information system and focus on analyzing and interpreting information.
    2. Enter the field with a college degree.
    3. Can achieve professional status as a **Certified Public Accountant (CPA)** and work for major accounting firms.
    4. The **controller** oversees the entire accounting process and is the principal accounting officer of a company.
    5. Services offered to other businesses by public accountants are as follows:
        a) **Auditing** involves reviewing companies' books to ensure correct policies and practices have been followed.
        b) **Taxation.** Tax specialists offer advice on tax planning, prepare tax returns, and represent clients before governmental agencies.
        c) **Management Advisory Services.** Offer advice to other businesses on a wide variety of managerial issues.
    6. Services offered by private accountants are as follows:
        a) **Accounting Information Services.** Design and implement manual and computerized accounting systems.
        b) **Financial Accounting.** Prepare various reports and financial statements.
        c) **Cost Accounting.** Record the cost of producing items. Analyze the production costs for efficiency.
        d) **Budgeting.** Help managers develop a financial plan.
        e) **Tax Accounting.** Internal tax accountant who focuses on tax planning, prepares tax returns, and deals with governmental agencies.
        f) **Internal Auditing.** Internal accountants who review the records to ensure correct policies and practices have been followed.
        g) **Certified Managerial Accountant.** A private accountant who gains professional status by passing a uniform examination offered by the Institute of Management Accounting.
        h) **Certified Internal Auditor.** A private accountant who gains professional status by passing a uniform examination offered by the Institute of Internal Auditors.

Teaching Tips

➤ The largest public accounting firms in the United States are known as the "Big Four." They are Deloitte and Touche, Ernst & Young, KPMG, and PricewaterhouseCoopers.

       7.   Governmental and not-for-profit accounting.
          a)   Accounting for states, cities, schools, churches, and hospitals.
          b)   Rules for governmental accounting somewhat different from for-profit companies.

VI.   Job Opportunities (**See Figure 1-6 and Figure 1-7**)
    A.   Job growth greater in some areas than others.
    B.   Computer skills needed to increase opportunities.
    C.   Writing skills needed by accountants.

Learning Activities

1. Have students identify several businesses in your community that are organized as sole proprietorships, partnerships, and corporations.

2. Have students identify several service, merchandising, and manufacturing businesses in your community.

Critical Thinking Activity

Have the students think of a business transaction such as buying stamps at the post office. Have the students explain how the transaction would affect all phases of the accounting process.

Homework Suggestions

LO1 Study Guide Review Question 1; End of Chapter Questions 1, 2.
LO2 Study Guide Review Question 11; End of Chapter Question 3.
LO3 Study Guide Review Question 7; End of Chapter Questions 4, 5.
LO4 Study Guide Review Questions 2, 3, 6, 9; End of Chapter Question 6.
LO5 Study Guide Review Questions 4, 5, 8; End of Chapter Question 7.
LO6 Study Guide Review Question 10; End of Chapter Questions 8, 9, 10.
Entire Chapter:
    Mastery Problem and Challenge Problem.

Ten Questions Your Students Will Always Ask

1. How much math is involved in accounting?
2. Can't computers do all this now?
3. Why is accounting required for my major?
4. Does one person perform all of the steps in the accounting process?
5. What do you mean by "liability"?
6. In a corporation, what is meant by liability being limited to initial investment?

7. Does that mean one partner can obligate his other partners, even if they did not know what he did?
8. How do you classify a restaurant?
9. What are the requirements for becoming a C.P.A.?
10. How much writing is involved in accounting?

Learning Objectives

LO1 Define the accounting elements.
LO2 Construct the accounting equation.
LO3 Analyze business transactions.
LO4 Show the effects of business transactions on the accounting equation.
LO5 Prepare an income statement, statement of owner's equity, and balance sheet.
LO6 Define the three basic phases of the accounting process.

LO1

Teaching Tip

➢ The definitions for the accounting elements are very important. Often students find memorizing definitions to be boring. Be sure to spend sufficient class time to ensure a solid understanding of these definitions. Throughout the course, students should be expected to be able to identify the accounting elements represented by the accounts used in transactions.

❖ **PowerPoint Slides 2-1 through 2-14 present The Accounting Elements**
❖ **Transparency Master 2-1 shows summary and financial statements**

I. The Accounting Elements
    A. **Business Entity** - the individual, association, or organization that engages in economic activities and controls specific resources.
    B. **Assets**
        1. Items owned by the business entity that will provide future benefits.
        2. Cash, merchandise, **accounts receivable**, and land are examples of assets.
    C. **Liabilities**
        1. Amounts owed to another business entity.
        2. **Accounts payable**—a promise to pay a supplier—and notes payable—formal written promises to pay a supplier or lender—are examples of liabilities.
    D. **Owner's Equity**
        1. The amount by which all assets exceed the business liabilities.
        2. The **net worth** of the business.
        3. Also called **capital**.
        4. The owner may have business assets/liabilities and non-business assets/liabilities. According to the **business entity concept,** non-business assets/liabilities must not be considered part of the business' records.

In-Class Exercise: Complete Exercise 2-1A, 2-1B (5 minutes each)

LO2

II.   The **Accounting Equation**
       A.   Assets = Liabilities + Owner's Equity

Teaching Tip

➢   The left side of the equation represents the assets. The right side of the equation shows where the money came from to buy the assets.

In-Class Exercise: Complete Exercise 2-2A, 2-2B (5 minutes each) and Problem 2-8A, 2-8B (5 minutes each)

LO3

III.   Analyzing **Business Transactions**
       A.   A business transaction is an exchange of at least two items of value.
       B.   All transactions affect at least two **accounts**, which are separate records used to summarize changes in each asset, liability, and owner's equity of the business.
       C.   **Account titles** provide a description of each type of account.
       D.   Three basic questions to answer for each transaction:
             1.   What happened?
             2.   Which accounts are affected?
                  a)   Identify the accounts affected.
                  b)   Classify the accounts.
             3.   How is the accounting equation affected?

LO4

IV.   Effect of Transactions on the Accounting Equation
       A.   Investment by owner
             1.   An increase in an asset is matched by an increase in owner's equity.
             2.   Increase in Cash and increase in Owner's Equity.

Teaching Tip

➢   Remember, Capital does not mean Cash. The cash is shown in the cash account.

       B.   Purchase of an asset for cash
             1.   Decrease in Cash.
             2.   Increase in asset (e.g., Delivery Equipment).

Teaching Tip

> Students often think that both sides of the accounting equation must be affected by a transaction. Point out that this is not true.

       C.   Purchase of an asset on account
           1.   Increase in the asset (e.g., Delivery Equipment).
           2.   Increase in the liability Accounts Payable.
       D.   Payment on account
           1.   Decrease in Cash.
           2.   Decrease in Accounts Payable.

In-Class Exercise: Complete Exercise 2-3A, 2-3B (10 minutes each)

❖   **PowerPoint Slides 2-52 through 2-60 present the Expanded Accounting Equation**

V.   Expanding the Accounting Equation: Revenue, Expenses, and Withdrawals
       A.   **Revenues**
           1.   The amount charged customers for goods and services.
           2.   Revenues increase assets.
           3.   Revenues increase owner's equity.

Teaching Tip

> Revenue is not Cash. Revenue is recorded when earned through the sale of a product or providing a service. If cash is received as a result, the cash account is increased. If not, another asset, Accounts Receivable, is increased.

       B.   Expenses
           1.   Created as a result of efforts made to produce revenues.
           2.   Expenses either decrease assets or increase liabilities.
           3.   Expenses reduce owner's equity.

Teaching Tips

> Students often confuse expenses and liabilities. Reinforce the definitions. An expense is the outflow of resources (decrease in assets or increase in liabilities) as a result of efforts made to produce revenues. The main purposes of recognizing an expense are to keep track of the amount and types of expenses incurred and to show the reduction in owner's equity. Note that an expense *can cause* a reduction in assets *or* an increase in liabilities. Wages earned by employees is a good example. If paid, the expense reduces an asset, cash. If not paid, it increases a liability, wages payable.

> Students often think that the expense account should be decreased when expenses are incurred. Stress that each time an expense is incurred, it is

9

recorded and added to the previous amount so that a total can be determined.

    C.   **Net income** or **net loss**
        1.   If revenues are larger than expenses, the business has a net income.
        2.   If revenues are smaller than expenses, the business has a net loss.
    D.   **Fiscal year**
        1.   Any accounting period for twelve consecutive months for which business records are kept.
        2.   The concept that income determination can be made on a periodic basis is the **accounting period concept**.
    E.   **Withdrawals** or **Drawing**
        1.   Amounts taken from the business by the owner for personal use.
        2.   Withdrawals reduce assets.
        3.   Withdrawals reduce owner's equity.

❖   **PowerPoint Slides 2-61 through 2-95 present the Effect of Revenue and Expenses on the Accounting Equation**

VI.   Effects of Revenue, Expense, and Withdrawal Transactions on the Accounting Equation (**See Figure 2-1**)
    A.   Delivery revenues earned in cash
        1.   Increase in Cash.
        2.   Increase in Delivery Fees which increases equity.
    B.   Paid rent for the month
        1.   Decrease in Cash.
        2.   Increase in Rent Expense which decreases equity.

Teaching Tip

➤   Students often think that expenses and drawing should have minus signs. Point out that as these items increase, owner's equity decreases.

    C.   Paid telephone bill
        1.   Decrease in Cash.
        2.   Increase in Telephone Expense which reduces equity.
    D.   Delivery revenues earned on account
        1.   Increase in Accounts Receivable (a claim to cash).
        2.   Increase in Delivery Fees which increases equity.
    E.   Purchase of supplies
        1.   Increase in Supplies.
        2.   Decrease in Cash.
    F.   Payment of insurance premium
        1.   Increase in Prepaid Insurance.
        2.   Decrease in Cash.

Teaching Tip

➤   If you think that the students are ready, you might mention that supplies and insurance used up during this accounting period will be recognized as expenses. These "adjustments" will be discussed later.

G. Receiving cash from prior services on account
    1. Increase in Cash.
    2. Decrease in Accounts Receivable.
H. Purchase of an asset on credit making a partial payment
    1. Increase in Equipment.
    2. Decrease in Cash.
    3. Increase in Accounts Payable.
I. Payment of wages
    1. Increase in Wages Expense which decreases equity.
    2. Decrease in Cash.
J. Deliveries made for cash and credit
    1. Increase in Cash.
    2. Increase in Accounts Receivable.
    3. Increase in Delivery Fees which increases equity.
K. Withdrawal of cash from the business.
    1. Increase in Drawing.
    2. Decrease in Cash.

Teaching Tip

➢   Point out that the owner does not receive a salary from the business. Cash
    or other assets are withdrawn to meet living expenses. The amount
    withdrawn depends on the personal needs of the owner. This amount may
    be more or less than net income in any given year.

In-Class exercise: Complete Exercise 2-4A, 2-4B (20 minutes each)
In-Class exercise: Complete Problem 2-9A, 2-9B (5 minutes each)

LO5

❖   **PowerPoint Slides 2-96 through 2-111 present Financial Statements**

VII.   Financial Statements

Teaching Tip

➢   It may be helpful to tell students that the headings to the financial statements
    answer three questions: Who? What? When?

❖   **Transparency Master 2-1 illustrates Figure 2-2 the Summary and Financial Statements.**

    A. **Income Statement (See Figure 2-2)**
        1. Sometimes called the **profit and loss statement** or **operating statement.**
        2. Reports the profitability of a business for a specific period of time.
        3. Revenue - expenses = net income or loss.

In-Class Exercise: Complete Problem 2-10A, 2-10B (10 minutes each)

    B. **Statement of Owner's Equity (See Figure 2-3)**
        1. Reports the activities in the owner's equity for a specific time period.

11

2.   Investments and profits increase capital.
3.   Withdrawals and losses decrease capital.

In-Class Exercise: Complete Exercise 2-6A, 2-6B, 2-7A, 2-7B (10 minutes each)
In-Class Exercise: Complete Problem 2-11A, 2-11B (15 minutes each)

    C.   **Balance Sheet**
        1.   Reports the assets, liabilities, and owner's equity on a given date.
        2.   Sometimes called a **statement of financial position** or **statement of financial condition.**
        3.   Assets = Liabilities + Owner's Equity

In-Class Exercise: Complete Problem 2-12A, 2-12B (10 minutes each)

    D.   Guidelines for Preparing Financial Statements
        1.   Standard formats should be used.
        2.   Headings should be used on all statements.
        3.   Single lines should be used to add or subtract numbers above the line.
        4.   Totals are double lined.
        5.   Dollar signs are used at the top of columns and beneath single (subtotal) rules.
        6.   Expenses may be listed from highest to lowest.
        7.   Assets are listed from most liquid to least liquid.

In-Class Exercise: Complete Exercise 2-5A, 2-5B (10 minutes each)

LO6

❖   **Transparency Master 2-2 illustrates Figure 2-4 Input, Processing, and Output.**
❖   **PowerPoint Slides 2-112 through 2-116 present same information**

VIII.   Overview of the Accounting Process **(See Figure 2-4)**
    A.   **Input.** Business transactions provide the necessary information for input.
    B.   **Processing.** Identifying, classifying, and determining how accounts are increased or decreased in business transactions.
    C.   **Output.** Recording the processed information on financial statements.

Learning Activities

1.   Ask the students to talk with the manager of a small business to identify the types of expenses in the business.

2.   Students should be able to know the difference between the six different types of accounts. Classifying accounts correctly in these early chapters is a must. The instructor should ask the students to give numerous examples of the types of accounts. Find out if the students know the difference between an asset and an expense.

Mark Hahn invested $26,000 in cash to open a law office on April 28 of the current year. On April 29, he purchased office equipment for $10,800. He paid cash for all but $1,550 of the office equipment. On April 30, Mark paid $1,200 for six months' insurance for his law practice. Mark wants to know his financial condition of the business as of April 30.

Solution

Mark Hahn, Attorney at Law
Balance Sheet
April 30, 20--

Assets		Liabilities	
Cash	$15,550	Accounts Payable	$ 1,550
Prepaid Insurance	1,200	Owner's Equity	
Office Equipment	10,800	Mark Hahn, Capital	$26,000
Total Assets	$27,550	Total Liab. and Own. Eq.	$27,550

Homework Suggestions

LO1 Study Guide Review Questions 2 through 7; End of Chapter Question 1.
LO2 Study Guide Review Questions 1, 8, 9, 10; Study Guide Exercises 1, 2, 4, 5; Study Guide Problem 12; End of Chapter Question 2.
LO3 End of Chapter Question 3.
LO4 Study Guide Review Questions 11 through 15; Study Guide Exercises 6, 7, 8; Study Guide Problem 13.
LO5 Study Guide Review Questions 16, 17, 18, 19; Study Guide Exercises 3, 9, 10, 11; Study Guide Problems 14, 15, 16, 17; End of Chapter Questions 4, 5, 6.
LO6 End of Chapter Question 7.
Entire Chapter:
Mastery Problem and Challenge Problem.

Ten Questions Your Students Will Always Ask

1. Can people be an asset?
2. Can an asset be something you cannot touch?
3. Is a lease you are obligated to pay a liability?
4. Do you always make two or more entries?
5. Is capital the same as cash?
6. Shouldn't liabilities be subtracted?
7. How do we keep track of different receipts of cash from different people who owe us?
8. Whom do we ask if we don't understand what a particular transaction means?
9. Do all businesses use these formal statements?
10. Isn't this an unwieldy approach to keeping track of transactions?

Learning Objectives

LO1 Define the parts of a T account.
LO2 Foot and balance a T account.
LO3 Describe the effects of debits and credits on specific types of accounts.
LO4 Use T accounts to analyze transactions.
LO5 Prepare a trial balance, and explain its purposes and linkages with the financial statements.

LO1

❖ **PowerPoint Slides 3-1 through 3-6 present the T Account**

I.   The T Account

Teaching Tip

➢ You might tell your students that other kinds of accounts will be illustrated later after the T accounts. However, T accounts are the most effective way to learn the double-entry system. Further, practicing accountants use them frequently when analyzing business transactions.

    A.   **Double-entry accounting** represents the fact that every transaction has a dual effect on the accounting equation.
    B.   Use T accounts to analyze transactions.
    C.   Each account has a title.
    D.   The left side is the **debit** side of each account.
    E.   The right side is the **credit** side of each account.

LO2

❖ **PowerPoint Slides 3-55 through 3-57 present Balancing T Accounts**

II.   Balancing a T Account **(See Figure 3-1)**

Teaching Tip

➢ Students may find it helpful to think of the T account like a balance beam scale. The heavier side will weight down the lighter side, so the balance is always written on the side with the larger or "heavier" footing.

    A.   **Footings.** Totals on the debit and credit sides.
    B.   **Balance.** Difference between the footings.
    C.   The balance is written on the side with the larger footing.

In-Class Exercise: Complete Exercise 3-1A, 3-1B (10 minutes each)

LO3

III.   Debits and Credits

Teaching Tip

➢   Emphasize to your students that debit simply means left and credit means right. They have heard about receiving credit. Often this has a positive connotation. Debit sounds like debt, which often has a negative impression. Tell them to forget about any positive or negative thoughts about debits and credits. They simply mean left and right—that to debit something simply means to put it on the left, to credit means to simply put it on the right.

A.   Debit means to enter an amount on the left side; credit means to enter an amount on the right side.

B.   Asset accounts
1.   Are on the left side of the accounting equation.
2.   Increases are entered on the debit, or left side.
3.   Decreases are entered on the credit, or right side.

C.   Liabilities and owner's equity accounts
1.   Are on the right side of the accounting equation.
2.   Increases are entered on the credit, or right side.
3.   Decreases are entered on the debit, or left side.

❖   **Transparency Master 3-1 illustrates Figure 3-2 Normal Balances.**

D.   **Normal balance (See Figure 3-2)**
1.   Is on the same side of an account that is increased.
2.   Asset accounts' normal balances are on the debit side; therefore, they have a **debit balance**.
3.   Liability accounts' and owner's equity normal balances are on the credit side; therefore, they have a **credit balance**.

❖   **Transparency Master 3-2 illustrates Figure 3-3 The Accounting Equation and the Owner's Equity Umbrella.**

E.   The owner's equity "umbrella" **(See Figure 3-3)**
1.   The accounting equation is Assets = Liabilities + Owner's Equity.
2.   The owner's equity "umbrella" includes capital, revenue, expense, and drawing accounts.

Teaching Tip

➢   Point out that since drawing and expenses decrease owner's equity, they are shown on the debit side of the umbrella. (Debits decrease owner's equity). As expenses and drawing increase (debits), owner's equity decreases. Revenue increases owner's equity and is shown on the credit side.

15

F. Revenue accounts
 1. Increases are recorded on the credit side.
 2. Decreases are recorded on the debit side.

❖ **Transparency Master 3-3 illustrates Figure 3-4 Normal Balances for the Owner's Equity Umbrella.**

 3. Have a normal credit balance. **(See Figure 3-4)**
G. Expense accounts
 1. Increases are recorded on the debit side.
 2. Decreases are recorded on the credit side.
 3. Have a normal debit balance. **(See Figure 3-4)**
H. Drawing account
 1. Increases are recorded on the debit side.
 2. Decreases are recorded on the credit side.
 3. Have a normal debit balance. **(See Figure 3-4)**

In-Class Exercise: Complete Exercises 3-2A, 3-2B, 3-4A, 3-4B (5 minutes each)

LO4

❖ **PowerPoint Slides 3-7 through 3-54 present Rules of Debits and Credits with Steps and Examples**

IV. Transaction Analysis **(See Figure 3-5)**

Teaching Tip

➢ Stress to your students that it is important to go through the three steps when analyzing transactions. The transaction must be fully understood before it can be accounted for correctly. Transactions in this chapter are easy to understand. Transactions in business can become quite complex, making this first step very important. Ultimately, students should strive to "see through" the transaction to determine its effects on the accounts, accounting equation, and, finally, the financial statements.

 A. Three basic questions
  1. What happened?
  2. Which accounts are affected?
   a) Identify the accounts.
   b) Classify the accounts.
  3. How is the accounting equation affected?
   a) Determine whether the accounts increased or decreased.
   b) Determine whether the accounts should be debited or credited.
   c) Make certain the accounting equation remains in balance after the transaction has been entered.
 B. Debits and credits: asset, liability, and owner's equity accounts

<u>Teaching Tip</u>

➢ The same transactions are used in both Chapter 2 and Chapter 3 in the chapter content. This allows students to focus on the new learning objectives: the double-entry framework.

    1. Investment by owner **(See Figure 3-6)**
       a) Increase in Cash is entered as a debit.
       b) Increase in Capital is entered as a credit.
    2. Purchase of an asset for cash. **(See Figure 3-7)**
       a) Increase in asset (e.g., Delivery Equipment) is entered as a debit.
       b) Decrease in Cash is entered as a credit.
    3. Purchase of an asset on account **(See Figure 3-8)**
       a) Increase in asset (e.g., Delivery Equipment) is entered as a debit.
       b) Increase in Accounts Payable is entered as a credit.
    4. Payment on a loan **(See Figure 3-9)**
       a) Decrease in Accounts Payable is entered as a debit.
       b) Decrease in Cash is entered as a credit.
  C. Debits and Credits: Including Revenues, Expenses, and Drawing **(See Figure 3-10)**
    1. Delivery revenues earned in cash **(See Figure 3-11)**
       a) Increase in Cash is entered as a debit.
       b) Increase in Delivery Fees is entered as a credit.
    2. Paid rent for the month **(See Figure 3-12)**

<u>Teaching Tip</u>

➢ Recall that expenses are debited because increases in expenses decrease owner's equity.

       a) Increase in Rent Expense is entered as a debit.
       b) Decrease in Cash is entered as a credit.
    3. Paid telephone bill **(See Figure 3-13)**
       a) Increase in Telephone Expense is entered as a debit.
       b) Decrease in Cash is entered as a credit.
    4. Delivery revenues are earned on account **(See Figure 3-14)**
       a) Increase in Accounts Receivable is entered as a debit.
       b) Increase in Delivery Fees is entered as a credit.
    5. Purchase of supplies **(See Figure 3-15)**
       a) Increase in the Supplies is entered as a debit.
       b) Decrease in Cash is entered as a credit.
    6. Payment of insurance premium **(See Figure 3-16)**
       a) Increase in Prepaid Insurance is entered as a debit.
       b) Decrease in Cash is entered as a credit.
    7. Received cash from prior sales on account **(See Figure 3-17)**
       a) Increase in Cash is entered as a debit.
       b) Decrease in Accounts Receivable is entered as a credit.
    8. Purchase of asset on credit making a partial payment **(See Figure 3-18)**
       a) Increase in asset (e.g., Delivery Equipment) is entered as a debit.
       b) Decrease in Cash is entered as a credit.
       c) Increase in Accounts Payable is entered as a credit.

9.   Payment of wages **(See Figure 3-19)**
      a)   Increase in Wages Expense is entered as a debit.
      b)   Decrease in Cash is entered as a credit.
10.   Deliveries made for cash and credit **(See Figure 3-20)**
      a)   Increase in Cash is entered as a debit.
      b)   Increase in Accounts Receivable is entered as a debit.
      c)   Increase in Delivery Fees in recorded as a credit.
11.   Withdrawal of cash from business **(See Figure 3-21)**
      a)   Increase in Drawing is entered as a debit.
      b)   Decrease in Cash is entered as a credit.

In-Class Exercise: Complete Exercise 3-3A, 3-3B, 3-5A, 3-5B (5-10 minutes each)
In-Class Exercise: Complete Exercise 3-6A, 3-6B (15 minutes each)

❖   **Transparency Master 3-4 illustrates Figure 3-22 Summary of Transactions (a) Through (o).**

V.   Summary of Transactions **(See Figure 3-22)**
    A.   Total each side of each T Account.
    B.   Write the totals (footings) in small numbers on each side of the T account.
    C.   The balance is shown on the side with the larger footing.
    D.   The footing serves as the balance for the accounts with entries on only one side of the account.
    E.   If an account has only a single entry, it is not necessary to enter a footing or balance.

In-Class Exercise: Complete Exercise 3-7A, 3-7B (10 minutes each)

LO5

❖   **PowerPoint Slides 3-58 through 3-65 present the Trial Balance**

VI.   The **Trial Balance (See Figure 3-23)**
    A.   Is prepared periodically to determine the equality of the debits and the credits.
    B.   Is a list of all accounts showing the title and balance of each account.
    C.   Provides proof that the
      1.   Total of the debits equals the total of the credits.
      2.   Accounting equation has remained in balance.

Teaching Tips

➤   Point out that the totals for the trial balance are not the same as those for the accounting equation. The trial balance compares the sum of all accounts with debit balances (assets, drawing, and expenses) with those with credit balances, (liabilities, owner's equity, and revenue). The accounting equation compares the sum of the asset accounts with the sum of the liabilities and owner's equity accounts using the expanded equation (Assets = Liabilities + Capital - Drawing + Revenue - Expenses).

➤   On financial statements, single rulings are used for amounts to be summed. Double rulings are used for totals.

> Dollar signs are not used on the trial balance. Remind students that dollar signs are used on financial statements at the top of each column and for the first amount entered in a column beneath a ruling.

In-Class Exercise: Complete Exercise 3-8A, 3-8B (10 minutes each)
In-Class Exercise: Complete Exercise 3-9A, 3-9B (10 minutes each)
In-Class Exercise: Complete Problem 3-13A, 3-13B (5 minutes each)

❖   **Transparency Master 3-5 illustrates Figure 3-24 Linkages Between the Trial Balance and Financial Statements.**

VIII.   Linkage between the Trial Balance and the Financial Statements **(See Figure 3-24)**
   A.   The trial balance is used as an aid in preparing the financial statements.

In-Class Exercise: Complete Exercise 3-10A, 3-10B (10 minutes each)
In-Class Exercise: Complete Exercise 3-11A, 3-11B (10 minutes each)
In-Class Exercise: Complete Exercise 3-12A, 3-12B (10 minutes each)
In-Class Exercise: Complete Problem 3-14A, 3-14B (5 minutes each)
In-Class Exercise: Complete Problem 3-15A, 3-15B (15 minutes each)

Learning Activities

1.   Emphasize debit means left and credit means right by having students raise their debit and credit hands, point to the debit and credit sides of the room, tell which hand they salute the flag with, etc.

2.   Have small groups of students develop an idea for a service business and prepare a list of assets, liabilities, revenues, and expenses. If similar businesses exist in your community, students can interview the owner or manager to identify the types of accounts used.

Critical Thinking Activities

1.   The business purchased delivery equipment in transactions (c) and (d) in the textbook. It paid cash in transaction (c) and purchased the equipment on account in transaction (d). Why didn't it just pay cash in both transactions?

Solution

It could not in transaction (d) because it would have reduced the cash to below zero. This could cause checks to bounce and cause harm to the reputation of the business. Even if the business had more cash, it may wish to purchase on account so there would be cash available for other uses.

2. The following accounts and their balances appear in the T accounts of the Deter Company:

Cash	$3,320
Supplies	250
Prepaid Insurance	980
Accounts Payable	1,000
Paul Deter, Capital	2,000
Delivery Fees	2,500
Rent Expense	500
Wages Expense	450

The owner prepared the trial balance that follows. The owner cannot get the totals to balance. Make a list of the errors that were made when the owner prepared the trial balance for the Deter Company.

Deter Company
Trail Balance
May 31, 20--

Account Title	Debit Balance	Credit Balance
Cash	3,320	
Supplies	250	
Prepaid Insurance	890	
Accounts Payable		1,000
Paul Deter, Capital		2,000
Delivery Fees		2,500
Rent Expense	500	
Wages Expense		450
	4,950	5,950

Solution

The Deter Company's owner made three mistakes in preparing the trial balance.
   1. They transposed the number for Prepaid Insurance. The number should be 980 not 890.
   2. Wages Expense was put in the credit column; should have been debited.
   3. The debit column was added incorrectly. The numbers should total to be $4,960, not $4,950.
   4. When all of these numbers are corrected, the total should be $5,500.

Homework Suggestions

LO1 Study Guide Review Questions 2, 3, 4; Study Guide Exercise 2; End of Chapter Questions 1, 2

LO2 Study Guide Review Questions 5, 6; End of Chapter Question 3

LO3 Study Guide Review Questions 7, 8, 10, 11, 12; Study Guide Exercises 1, 3; End of Chapter Question 4

LO4 Study Guide Review Question 1; Study Guide Exercises 4, 5, 6, 7

LO5 Study Guide Review Question 9; Study Guide Exercise 8; Study Guide Problem 9; End of Chapter Question 5

Entire Chapter:
Study Guide Problems 10, 11; Mastery Problem and Challenge Problem.

Ten Questions Your Students Will Always Ask

1. Is this what they mean by "double-entry" bookkeeping?
2. Why are assets "debits" when my checkbook says when I deposit money I "credit" my account?
3. Is there any aid we can use to remember all this?
4. Do we still have to make sure each transaction balances?
5. Why is something we use up—like pencils—an asset?
6. Do actual businesses really do it this way?
7. Does "paid" always mean cash out—a credit?
8. Does "received" a bill always mean a liability—a credit?
9. What if the boss takes his personal assistant to lunch—an expense or a withdrawal?
10. Do we always have to be so particular about form on the financial statements?

Learning Objectives

LO1 Describe the flow of data from source documents through the trial balance.
LO2 Describe the chart of accounts as a means of classifying financial information.
LO3 Describe and explain the purpose of source documents.
LO4 Journalize transactions.
LO5 Post to the general ledger and prepare a trial balance.
LO6 Explain how to find and correct errors.

LO1

❖ Transparency Master 4-1 illustrates Figure 4-1 Flow of Data from Source Documents through Trial Balance.
❖ PowerPoint Slides 4-1 through 4-3 present the same information

I. Flow of Data **(See Figure 4-1)**
    A.   Analyze transactions using source documents and chart of accounts.
    B.   Enter transactions in the general journal.
    C.   Post entries to the account in the ledger.
    D.   Prepare a trial balance from the general ledger.

LO2

❖ Transparency Master 4-2 illustrates Figure 4-2 Chart of Accounts.
❖ PowerPoint Slides 4-4 through 4-10 present the same information

II. The **Chart of Accounts (See Figure 4-2)**
    A.   Asset accounts begin with "1"
    B.   Liability accounts begin with "2"
    C.   Owner's equity accounts begin with "3"
    D.   Revenue accounts begin with "4"
    E.   Expense accounts begin with "5"

Teaching Tips

➢ Point out the chart of accounts on the inside back cover of the text.

➢ Encourage your students to use the chart of accounts order for listing expenses on the income statement. This is often easier than listing by amount when doing the homework.

➢ Most accounting software contains a standard chart of accounts. You might bring one in and briefly explain that all charts are organized in a systematic manner.

LO3

❖   **PowerPoint Slides 4-11 through 4-13 present Source Documents**

III.   **Source documents (See Figure 4-3)**
- A.   These trigger the analysis of what has happened.
- B.   They serve as evidence to verify the accuracy of accounting records.

In-Class Exercise: Complete Exercise 4-1A, 4-1B (5 minutes each)

Teaching Tip

➢   Emphasize that source documents provide objective, verifiable evidence of the transaction. These documents could be important if anyone challenges the accuracy of the accounting records.

LO4

❖   **PowerPoint Slides 4-14 through 4-32 present the General Journal**

IV.   The **General Journal**
- A.   Referred to as a **book of original entry**
  1.   It is here that the first formal accounting record of a transaction is made.
  2.   It shows the date of each transaction, title of the account to be debited and the account to be credited, and the amounts of the debit and credit.

Teaching Tip

➢   Perhaps comparing the journal to a diary or log would be helpful.

       3.   **Compound entry -** a general journal entry that affects more than two accounts, thus having more than one debit and/or one credit.

❖   **Transparency Master 4-3 illustrates Figure 4-4 Two-Column General Journal.**

- B.   **Two-column general journal (See Figure 4-4)**

  1.   Named because it has only two amount columns, one for debit amounts and one for credit amounts.
  2.   Contents **(See Figure 4-5)**
     - a)   Date column
     - b)   Description column
       - (1)   Accounts to be debited are listed first.
       - (2)   Accounts to be credited are indented and listed after the debits.
     - c)   Posting Reference column
     - d)   Debit column amount
     - e)   Credit column amount
     - f)   Skip a line between entries
- C.   **Journalizing (See Figure 4-6 and Figure 4-7)**

Teaching Tips

➤ The transactions introduced for Jessie Jane's Delivery are repeated in this chapter. This will allow the student to focus on the new topics to be learned: journalizing and posting.

➤ Remind your students of the three main questions to ask when analyzing a transaction:
1. What happened?
2. Which accounts are affected?
   - Classify these accounts as assets, liabilities, owner's equity, revenue, or expenses.
3. How is the accounting equation affected?
   - Determine whether the accounts have increased or decreased.
   - Determine whether the accounts should be debited or credited.

      1.   Act of entering transactions in a journal.
           a)   Date
           b)   Title of each account
           c)   Amounts
           d)   Brief description
      2.   Four-step process is repeated for each transaction.

Teaching Tips

➤ Stress using the proper format and account titles when entering transactions in the journal.

➤ Sometimes students think that dollar signs should be used in the journal and ledger. Explain that dollar signs are used only on formal reports and financial statements.

➤ Remind your students that supplies and prepaid insurance are assets because they provide future benefits. The supplies purchased June 16 will last more than one month and the insurance premium paid June 18 covers eight months. Some students might ask when an expense will be recognized. Encourage them to hold on. This will be discussed in Chapter 5.

➤ Students sometimes have a difficult time remembering the exact account titles. Although this is understandable, the account titles listed in the firm's chart of accounts must be used for journalizing. With practice, using proper account titles will seem easy.

In-Class Exercise: Complete Exercise 4-2A, 4-2B (10 minutes each)

LO5

❖   **PowerPoint Slides 4-33 through 4-42 present the General Ledger**

V.   The **General Ledger**

<u>Teaching Tip</u>

➢   Stress that the journal and ledger are different books.

    A.   It provides a complete record of the transactions entered into each account.
    B.   Accounts are numbered and arranged in the same order as the chart of accounts.

❖   **Transparency Master 4-4 illustrates Figure 4-8 Comparison of T Account and Four-Column Account.**

    C.   **Four-column account (See Figure 4-8)**
        1.   Date column
        2.   Item column

<u>Teaching Tip</u>

➢   The "Item" column is also used to identify adjusting and closing entries made at the end of the accounting period. This will be discussed in Chapters 5 and 6.

        3.   Posting Reference column
        4.   Debit entry column
        5.   Credit entry column
        6.   Debit balance column
        7.   Credit balance column
        8.   Heading has the account title and the account number

❖   **Transparency Master 4-5 illustrates Figure 4-9 Posting a Debit.**

❖   **Transparency Master 4-6 illustrates Figure 4-10 Posting a Credit.**

    D.   **Posting** to the General Ledger **(See Figure 4-9 and Figure 4-10)**

<u>Teaching Tip</u>

➢   Point out that transactions should be entered in the journal as they occur. However, posting can wait until enough transactions have accumulated to use posting time efficiently. Of course, all transactions must be entered and posted prior to preparing financial statements.

1. Steps
   a) Enter the date of the transaction in the Date column.
   b) Enter the amount of the debit or credit in the Debit or Credit column.
   c) Enter the new balance in the Balance columns under debit or credit.

Teaching Tip

➢ Encourage your students to double check their math as they go along. This can save hours of searching for an error later.

   d) Enter the journal page number from which each transaction is posted in the Posting Reference column.
   e) Enter the ledger account number in the Posting Reference column of the journal for each transaction that is posted.

Teaching Tip

➢ Posting is mechanical. The transactions do not need to be analyzed again. In computerized accounting systems, the posting is done automatically by the computer.

❖ **Transparency Master 4-7 illustrates Figure 4-11 General Journal After Posting.**

❖ **Transparency Master 4-8 illustrates Figure 4-12 General Ledger After Posting.**

2. **Cross referencing** in the posting reference columns of the journal and the ledger provides a link between journal and the ledger **(See Figure 4-11 and Figure 4-12)**

In-Class Exercise: Complete Exercise 4-3A, 4-3B (15 minutes each)

❖ **PowerPoint Slides 4-43 and 4-44 present the Trial Balance**

E. **Trial Balance (See Figure 4-13)**
   1. It is used to prove the equality of the debits and credits in the ledger accounts.
   2. Transactions should be all posted and journalized before the trial balance is prepared.
   3. Accounts are listed in the order used in the chart of accounts.

Teaching Tips

➢ To determine the final account balance when posting, use the following chart:

Account Balance	Posted Amount	Math
Debit	Debit	Add
Debit	Credit	Subtract
Credit	Debit	Subtract
Credit	Credit	Add

➢ Students should be reminded that journalizing and posting are not just doing activities. They are thinking processes as well. Journalizing can be an automatic process once the student gains some experience. This is the time when mistakes are often made. Don't take any part of this process for granted. The explanation is a perfect example. The student may think the explanations listed after each transaction in this chapter just repeat the transaction. Explanations are given for the readers of the general journal as well. They may provide information or computations which clarify the transaction.

➢ Be sure to show your students the linkage between the trial balance and the ledger account. Have them flip back to the ledger accounts to see that the balance of each account was copied to the trial balance.

In-Class Exercise: Complete Exercise 4-5A, 4-5B (20 minutes each)
In-Class Exercise: Complete Exercise 4-6A, 4-6B (15 minutes each)
In-Class Exercise: Complete Exercise 4-7A, 4-7B (15 minutes each)

LO6

❖ **PowerPoint Slides 4-45 through 4-65 present Finding and Correcting Errors in the Trial Balance**

VI. Finding and Correcting Errors in the Trial Balance
    A. Finding Errors **(See Figure 4-14)**
        1. Double check your addition.
        2. Find the difference between the debits and credits.
            a) Check for missing debits and credits if the error is the same as the transaction.
            b) Divide the difference by 2. It could mean two debits and no credits, or vice versa.
            c) Divide the difference by 9.
                (1) Could mean a **transposition error.**
                (2) Could mean a **slide error.**
                (3) Retrace your steps through the accounting process checking postings.
    B. Correcting Errors

❖ **Transparency Master 4-9 illustrates Figure 4-15 Ruling Method of Making a Correction.**

1. **Ruling method (See Figure 4-15)**
   a)   Used to correct two types of errors.
      (1)   Incorrect journal entry has been made, but not posted.
      (2)   Proper entry has been made but posted incorrectly.
   b)   Using the ruling method
      (1)   Draw a line through the incorrect account title or amount.
      (2)   Write the correct information directly above the ruling.
      (3)   Initial the correction.

❖   **Transparency Master 4-10 illustrates Figure 4-16 Correcting Entry Method.**

2. **Correcting entry method (See Figure 4-16)**
   a)   Used when an incorrect entry has been journalized and posted to the wrong account.
   b)   Using the correcting entry method
      (1)   Make an entry in the general journal to reverse the original entry.
      (2)   Include an explanation.

❖   **Transparency Master 4-11 illustrates Figure 4-17 Effects of Correcting Entry on Ledger Accounts.**

      (3)   Post to the related general ledger accounts **(See Figure 4-17)**

In-Class Exercise: Complete Exercise 4-8A, 4-8B (10 minutes each)
In-Class Exercise: Complete Problem 4-11A, 4-11B (10 minutes each)

Learning Activities

1.   In earlier chapters, students developed an idea for a business. Ask the students to develop a chart of accounts for that business.

2.   Ask students to make a list of the source documents that they have for their own personal transactions and to bring samples of these documents to class.

Critical Thinking Activities

1.   The chart of accounts is like any numbering system in that it is a process of grouping data in a specific way. To demonstrate this, ask students to list various numbering systems and define what type of data the system is used to organize. For example, the Dewey Decimal system is a way of organizing books in a library. Street addresses are a way of identifying specific houses on a street.

2.   Ask students to prepare a chart of accounts for a business of their own choosing or to use the chart of accounts prepared in Learning Activity 1. Then ask them to list two source documents that could be used as evidence of amounts shown in those accounts. The instructor should emphasize the importance of source documents. If the business is audited, the source documents may be used to prove the numbers on the tax return.

Examples:

> Cash - check stubs and bank statement
> Supplies - canceled check and receipt of payment
> Prepaid Insurance - canceled check and policy
> Vehicle - purchase agreement and title
> Rent Expense - canceled check and lease agreement

Homework Suggestions

LO1 Study Guide Review Question 4; End of Chapter Question 1

LO2 Study Guide Review Questions 1, 2, 3; End of Chapter Questions 2, 3

LO3 End of Chapter Question 4

LO4 Study Guide Review Questions 5, 6, 7, 8, 9; Study Guide Exercise 1, 2; End of Chapter Questions 5, 6; Exercise 4-4A, 4-4B

LO5 Study Guide Review Questions 10, 11, 12, 13, 14, 15; Study Guide Exercises 3, 4; Study Guide Problems 5, 6; End of Chapter Questions 7, 8, 9, 10; Problems 4-9A, 4-9B, 4-10A, 4-10B

LO6 Study Guide Review Questions 16, 17, 18, 19; Study Guide Problem 7; End of Chapter Questions 11, 12, 13, 14, 15

Entire Chapter:

Mastery Problem and Challenge Problem, Study Guide Exercise 1.

Ten Questions Your Students Will Always Ask

1. Is all of this work really necessary?
2. Are source documents always provided to the bookkeeper/accountant?
3. Do we have to memorize the chart of accounts numbers?
4. Must you always journalize debits first?
5. Do we have to enter the explanation, even if the entry is obvious?
6. What is the difference between the general ledger and the general journal?
7. In a ledger account, do you balance every time?
8. How often do you post?
9. If my trial balance does not balance, where should I look first?
10. Which method should I use to correct an error if my handwriting is sloppy?

Learning Objectives

LO1 Prepare end-of-period adjustments.
LO2 Prepare a work sheet.
LO3 Describe methods for finding errors on the work sheet.
LO4 Journalize adjusting entries.
LO5 Post adjusting entries to the general ledger.

Teaching Tip

➢ This is a good time to review GAAP. Reviewing the various concepts and principles from the investor/creditor viewpoint may make GAAP's purpose clearer.

LO1

❖ **PowerPoint Slides 5-1 through 5-42 present End of Period Adjustments**

I. End-of-Period Adjustments
   A. **Matching principle** requires accounts to be brought up to date before financial statements are prepared.
      1. Reasons to adjust the trial balance **(See Figure 5-1 and Figure 5-2)**
         a) Report all revenue earned.
         b) Report all expenses incurred.
         c) Report accurately the assets that have been used up.
         d) Report accurately the liabilities that have been incurred but not yet paid.
   B. **Fiscal year** end
      1. Accounting year ends.
         a) Calendar year
         b) Month end other than December 31
      2. Adjustments are made and financial statements are prepared.
   C. Types of Adjusting Entries

Teaching Tips

➢ You might want to point out that all adjusting entries addressed in this text, and at the introductory level in general, will affect both the income statement and balance sheet. In fact, we can think of only one adjustment that affects the balance sheet only. This adjustment, which is for unrealized gains or losses on available-for-sale securities, is generally addressed in intermediate accounting.

> To determine the adjusting entry for supplies, first compute the amount of supplies used.

Supplies available:	80
Supplies left:	-20
Supplies used:	60

The amount used is an expense and reduces the amount that should be reported as an asset.

❖ **Transparency Master 5-1 illustrates Figure 5-3 Adjustment for Supplies.**

❖ **Transparency Master 5-2 illustrates Figure 5-4 Effect of Adjusting Entry for Supplies on Financial Statements.**

    1.   Supplies **(See Figure 5-3 and Figure 5-4)**
        a)   Adjust the supplies used.
        b)   Debit Supplies Expense and credit Supplies.

In-Class Exercise: Complete Exercise 5-1A, 5-1B, 5-6A, 5-6B (5 minutes each)

Teaching Tip

> The analysis for prepaid insurance is very similar to that used for supplies. First, compute the amount of insurance that expired. This amount is an expense and reduces the amount that should be reported as an asset.

❖ **Transparency Master 5-3 illustrates Figure 5-5 Adjustment for Expired Insurance.**

❖ **Transparency Master 5-4 illustrates Figure 5-6 Effect of Adjusting Entry for Prepaid Insurance on Financial Statements.**

    2.   Prepaid insurance **(See Figure 5-5 and Figure 5-6)**
        a)   Adjust the amount of insurance expired.
        b)   Debit Insurance Expense and credit Prepaid Insurance.

In-Class Exercise: Complete Exercise 5-2A, 5-2B, 5-7A, 5-7B (5 minutes each)

Teaching Tip

> Students may wonder how a wage expense was incurred without making the payment. Point out that most businesses pay their employees on the same day each week or month. If the employees are paid on Fridays and the end of the accounting period is on a Tuesday, any wages earned on Saturday, Sunday, Monday, and Tuesday will be paid on the next Friday. The next Friday is in a new accounting period. Since the wages were earned in the original accounting period, they should be recognized as an expense and a liability because the wages were not paid yet.

❖   Transparency Master 5-5 illustrates Figure 5-7 Adjustment for Unpaid Wages.

❖   Transparency Master 5-6 illustrates Figure 5-8 Effect of Adjusting Entry for Wages on Financial Statements for June.

       3.   Accrued wages **(See Figure 5-7 and Figure 5-8)**
            a)   Adjust wages owed but not yet paid.
            b)   Debit Wages Expense and credit Wages Payable.

In-Class Exercise: Complete Exercise 5-3A, 5-3B (5 minutes each)

Teaching Tip

➤   The Appendix to Chapter 5 addresses other depreciation methods.

❖   Transparency Master 5-7 illustrates Figure 5-9 Effect of Adjustment for Depreciation of Delivery Equipment.

❖   Transparency Master 5-8 illustrates Figure 5-10 Effect of Adjusting Entry for Depreciation on Financial Statements for June.

❖   Transparency Master 5-9 illustrates figure 5-11 Effect of Adjusting Entry for Depreciation on Financial Statements for July.

       4.   **Depreciation** expense **(See Figure 5-9, Figure 5-10, and Figure 5-11)**
            a)   Adjust the cost of durable assets which provide benefits over a long period of time (**plant assets**).

Teaching Tip

➤   "Contra" means against or opposite. Thus, a contra-asset account has the opposite balance of an asset. The asset and contra-asset should be viewed together. The asset account, Equipment, shows the historical cost of equipment. The contra-asset, Accumulated Depreciation-Equipment, shows that portion of the original cost that has been used up.

            b)   Debit Depreciation Expense and credit the **contra-asset** Accumulated Depreciation.
            c)   Assets are recorded at cost under the **historical cost principle**.
            d)   Assets are depreciated over their useful lives using the **straight-line method** (Cost - **Salvage Value**) ÷ Estimated **Useful Life**. The **depreciable cost** is the original cost less the salvage value.

Teaching Tip

➤   Stress the difference between depreciable cost and book value.
       Depreciable cost = Cost - Salvage Value
       Book Value = Cost - Accumulated Depreciation

            e)   **Book value** or **undepreciated cost** is the difference between cost and accumulated depreciation.

<u>Teaching Tip</u>

➤ Book value is not the same as market value. Depreciation shows that a portion of the asset's useful life has expired. A portion of the depreciable cost is matched against the revenues that the asset helped produce. The book value is not intended to represent the selling price of the asset.

        f)   Book value does not represent the selling price, which is also referred to as **market value**.

In-Class Exercise: Complete Exercise 5-4A, 5-4B, 5-5A, 5-5B (10 minutes each)

❖   **Transparency Master 5-10 illustrates Figure 5-12 Expanded Chart of Accounts.**

    D.   Expanded Chart of Accounts **(See Figure 5-12)**
        1.   New accounts are added when adjusting entries are made.
        2.   Contra accounts carry the same number as the related asset account with a ".1" suffix.

LO2

❖   **PowerPoint Slides 5-43 through 5-78 present the Work Sheet**

II.   The **Work Sheet**
    A.   Pulls together all of the information needed to enter adjusting entries and prepare the financial statements.

<u>Teaching Tip</u>

➤ Emphasize that the work sheet is a tool used by the accountant. None of the adjustments made on the work sheet have any effect on the accounts unless the entries are made in the journal.

    B.   The Ten-Column Work Sheet
        1.   Heading
            a)   Name of the company
            b)   Work Sheet
            c)   Date when the accounting period ends
        2.   Amount column headings
            a)   Trial Balance
            b)   Adjustments
            c)   Adjusted Trial Balance
            d)   Income Statement
            e)   Balance Sheet

Teaching Tips

➢ Point out that the work sheet does not have columns for the statement of owner's equity. Drawing is placed as a debit in the Balance Sheet columns, and net income is calculated as the difference between the debits and credits in the Income Statement and Balance Sheet columns.

➢ The novice accounting student often struggles to prepare work sheets. Review the contents of the five sets of amount columns on the work sheet. Stress what each column should contain. Students seem to have the most difficulty in taking numbers from the Adjusted Trial Balance column to the Income Statement and Balance Sheet columns. Remind students that the Income Statement columns contain revenue and expenses (items appearing on the income statement). The difference will be net income or loss. The Balance Sheet columns contain Assets, Drawing, Liabilities, and Owner's Capital. Assigning a take-home test removes the time pressure and encourages students to be more thorough in their work.

➢ Tips for assuring accuracy when preparing a work sheet are as follows:
  • Check the equality of the trial balance columns BEFORE making adjustments.
  • Check the equality of the adjustment debits and credits BEFORE extending any accounts.
  • Use a ruler when extending balances. This will help you avoid inserting amounts on the wrong line.
  • Remember: net income, apart; net loss, together.

❖ **Transparency Master 5-11 illustrates Figure 5-13 Steps in Preparing the Work Sheet.**

C.   Preparing the Work Sheet **(See Figure 5-13)**

❖ **Transparency Master 5-12 illustrates Figure 5-14 Step 1—Prepare the Trial Balance.**

1.   Prepare the Trial Balance. **(See Figure 5-14)**

❖ **Transparency Master 5-13 illustrates Figure 5-15 Step 2—Prepare the Adjustments.**

2.   Prepare the Adjustments. **(See Figure 5-15)**

In-Class Exercise: Complete Exercise 5-8A, 5-8B (15 minutes each)

❖ **Transparency Master 5-14 illustrates Figure 5-16 Step 3—Prepare the Adjusted Trial Balance.**

3. Prepare the **Adjusted Trial Balance**. (See Figure 5-16)

❖   **Transparency Master 5-15 illustrates Figure 5-17 Step 4—Extend Adjusted Balances to the Income Statement and Balance Sheet Columns.**

       4.   Extend adjusted balances to Income Statement and Balance Sheet columns. **(See Figure 5-17)**

          a)   **Income Statement columns**

             (1)   Revenue accounts are extended to the Income Statement Credit column.

             (2)   Expense accounts are extended to the Income Statement Debit column.

          b)   **Balance Sheet columns**

             (1)   Asset and drawing accounts are extended to the Balance Sheet Debit column.

             (2)   Liabilities and owner's equity are extended to the Balance Sheet Credit column.

❖   **Transparency Master 5-16 illustrates Figure 5-18 Step 5—Complete the Work Sheet.**

       5.   Complete the Work Sheet **(See Figure 5-18)**

          a)   Total the Income Statement columns. **(See Figure 5-19)**

             (1)   Net income: total of the credits (revenue) exceeds the total of the debits (expenses).

             (2)   Net loss: total of the debits exceeds the total of the credits.

          b)   Total the Balance Sheet columns.

             (1)   The difference between the totals of the columns is the amount of net income or net loss.

             (2)   Difference should be the same as the difference found for the Income Statement columns.

             (3)   Columns should be double ruled once the columns are balanced.

In-Class Exercise: Complete Exercise 5-10A, 5-10B, 5-11A, 5-11B (10 minutes each)

LO3

❖   **PowerPoint Slides 5-79 and 5-80 present Finding Errors on the Work Sheet**

III.   Finding Errors on the Work Sheet **(See Figure 5-20)**

       A.   Check the addition of all columns.

       B.   Check the addition and subtraction required when extending to the Adjusted Trial Balance columns.

       C.   Make sure the adjusted account balances have been extended to the appropriate columns.

       D.   Make sure that the net income or loss has been added to the appropriate columns.

In-Class Exercise: Complete Problem 5-16A, 5-16B (15 minutes each)

LO4

❖ **Transparency Master 5-17 illustrates Figure 5-21 Adjusting Entries.**
❖ **PowerPoint Slides 5-81 through 5-85 present the same information**

IV. Journalizing Adjusting Entries (**See Figure 5-21**)
    A.   Copy the adjustments from the work sheet to the journal.
    B.   Journalize the adjustments on the year-end date.
    C.   Write "Adjusting Entries" in the Description column for individual adjusting entries.

In-Class Exercise: Complete Exercise 5-9A, 5-9B (15 minutes each)

LO5

❖ **Transparency Master 5-18 illustrates Figure 5-22 Posting the Adjusting Entry for Supplies.**
❖ **PowerPoint Slides 5-86 and 5-87 present the same information**

V. Posting Adjusting Entries (**See Figure 5-22**)
    A.   Post to the general ledger in the same manner as all other entries.
    B.   Write "Adjusting" in the Item column of the general ledger.

In-Class Exercise: Complete Exercise 5-12A, 5-12B (15 minutes each)

Learning Activity

For the business that you have developed, list the equipment, furniture, tools, and buildings that the business might own. Estimate the useful lives of these items. Consider the fact that a building would likely last longer than an automobile. Also list reasons the assets' useful lives will expire. For example, miles driven cause engine wear in an automobile.

Critical Thinking Activity

Have students list major assets they own. For each asset (stereo, car, etc.) have students calculate depreciation. Discuss what facts must be known and what assumptions must be made.

Homework Suggestions

LO1   Study Guide Review Questions 1 through 10; Study Guide Exercises 1, 2; End of Chapter Questions 1 through 8
LO2   Study Guide Review Questions 11 through 16; Study Guide Problems 6, 7; End of Chapter Questions 9, 10, 11; Problems 5-13A, 5-13B, 5-14A. 5-14B
LO3   Study Guide Problem 8; End of Chapter Question 12
LO4   Combined with LO5 Homework
LO5   Study Guide Exercises 3, 4, 5; End of Chapter Problem 5-15A, 5-15B
Entire Chapter:
    Mastery Problem and Challenge Problem

1.   We adjust only at the end of the accounting period, correct?
2.   Why are we given two kinds of figures—amount used or amount on hand?
3.   Why don't we just total up the paychecks we write each accounting period?
4.   Who determines the lifetime of a machine?
5.   What about machines that are still serviceable after their predetermined useful life has expired?
6.   Are all work sheets this big?
7.   Is the adjusted trial balance the sum of the trial balance and the adjustments columns?
8.   When do we journalize the adjustments?
9.   What is the effect of a repair on a machine?
10. Why doesn't everyone use the MACRS system since the IRS uses it?

Learning Objectives

LO1 Prepare a depreciation schedule using the straight-line method.
LO2 Prepare a depreciation schedule using the sum-of-the-years'-digits method.
LO3 Prepare a depreciation schedule using the double-declining-balance method.
LO4 Prepare a depreciation schedule for tax purposes using the Modified Accelerated Cost Recovery System.

LO1

❖ Transparency Master 5-19 illustrates Figure 5A-1 Depreciation Schedule Using Straight-Line Method.
❖ PowerPoint Slides 5Apx-1 through 5Apx-19 present the same information

I. Straight-Line Method **(See Figure 5A-1)**
    A. Equal amount of depreciation will be taken each period.
    B. Depreciation expense for one year = (Cost - Salvage Value) ÷ Years of Life.
    C. Rate of depreciation = 100% ÷ years of life.
    D. Depreciation schedule is prepared showing the depreciation expense, accumulated depreciation, and book value for each year.

In-Class Exercise: Complete Exercise 5Apx-1A, 5Apx-1B (10 minutes each)

LO2

❖ Transparency Master 5-20 illustrates Figure 5A-2 Depreciation Schedule Using Sum-of-the-Years'-Digits Method.
❖ PowerPoint Slides 5Apx-20 through 5Apx-36 present the same information

II. Sum-of-the-Years'-Digits Method **(See Figure 5A-2)**
    A. A larger amount of depreciation is taken in the early years of the asset
    B. Depreciation expense for one year = Depreciable Cost × Pre-determined fraction.
        1. Numerator for fraction is the number of years of remaining useful life, measured from the beginning of the year.
        2. Denominator for all fractions is determined by adding the digits of the years of useful life. (Example: 5 year asset would be 5 + 4 + 3 + 2 + 1)

In-Class Exercise: Complete Exercise 5Apx-2A, 5Apx-2B (15 minutes each)

LO3

❖ **Transparency Master 5-21 illustrates Figure 5A-3 Depreciation Schedule Using Double-Declining-Balance Method.**

❖ **PowerPoint Slides 5Apx-37 through 5Apx-52 present the same information**

III. Double-Declining-Balance Method **(See Figure 5A-3)**
   A. A larger amount of depreciation is taken in the early years of the asset.
   B. Depreciation expense for one year = Book Value × fixed rate
      1. Fixed rate = (1 ÷ years of useful life) × 2

In-Class Exercise: Complete Exercise 5Apx-3A, 5Apx-3B (15 minutes each)

LO4

❖ **Transparency Master 5-22 illustrates Figure 5A-4 Depreciation Schedule Using Modified Accelerated Cost Recovery System.**

❖ **PowerPoint Slides 5Apx-53 through 5Apx-62 present the same information**

IV. Modified Accelerated Cost Recovery System **(See Figure 5A-4)**
   A. Used to determine depreciation for tax purposes.
   B. Used for assets purchased after 1986.
   C. Internal Revenue Service (IRS) classifies various assets according to useful life.
   D. IRS sets depreciation rates for each year of assets' lives.
   E. Depreciation expense for one year = Cost × IRS Fixed Rate

In-Class Exercise: Complete Exercise 5Apx-4A, 5Apx-4B (10 minutes each)

Homework Suggestions

LO1 Study Guide Apx Exercise 1
LO2 Study Guide Apx Exercise 2
LO3 Study Guide Apx Exercise 3
LO4 Study Guide Apx Exercise 4

Learning Objectives

LO1   Prepare financial statements with the aid of a work sheet.
LO2   Journalize and post closing entries.
LO3   Prepare a post-closing trial balance.
LO4   List and describe the steps in the accounting cycle.

LO1

❖   **Transparency Master 6-1 illustrates Figure 6-1 Linkages Between the Work Sheet and Income Statement**

❖   **Transparency Master 6-2 illustrates Figure 6-2 Linkages Between the Work Sheet, Statement of Owner's Equity, and Balance Sheet**

❖   **PowerPoint Slides 6-1 through 6-4 present the Work Sheet as Information Source for Financial Statements**

I.   The Financial Statements **(See Figure 6-1 and Figure 6-2)**
     A.   Appearance
          1.   Dollar signs are placed at the top of each column and beneath rulings.
          2.   Single rulings indicate addition or subtraction.
          3.   Double rulings are placed under totals.
          4.   Headings contain
               a)   Company name
               b)   Statement title
               c)   Period ended or date

Teaching Tip

➢   Remind the students that the headings of financial statements relate to who, what, and when.

❖   **PowerPoint Slides 6-5 through 6-16 present the Income Statement**

     B.   The Income Statement

Teaching Tip

➢   Remind the students that the work sheet was used to prepare adjusting entries in Chapter 5.

          1.   Income Statement columns of the work sheet provide the information needed to prepare the income statement.
          2.   Revenues are listed first.

3. Expenses are listed next.
    a) They could be listed in the order that they appear in the chart of accounts.
    b) They could be listed in descending order by dollar amount.
    c) Amounts are itemized in the left column.
    d) Subtotals appear in the right column.
4. Revenues - expenses = net income or net loss.

❖ **PowerPoint Slides 6-17 through 6-25 present the Statement of Owner's Equity**

C. The Statement of Owner's Equity
   1. Information is taken from
    a) Balance sheet columns of the worksheet.
    b) Beginning owner's equity.
    c) Drawing account.
    d) Net income or net loss from the income statement.

In-Class Exercise: Complete Exercise 6-2A, 6-2B (10 minutes each)

   2. Additional investments would be added to the beginning equity balance.

Teaching Tip

➢ If additional investments are not reported on the statement of owner's equity, the beginning balance of owner's equity for the current period will not be the same as the ending balance for owner's equity from the prior period.

❖ **Transparency Master 6-3 illustrates Figure 6-3 Statement of Owner's Equity with Additional Investment.**

   3. Beginning owner's equity + additional investments + net income (or - net loss) - withdrawals = ending owner's equity. **(See Figure 6-3)**

In-Class Exercise: Complete Problem 6-7A, 6-7B (10 minutes each)

❖ **PowerPoint Slides 6-26 through 6-45 present the Balance Sheet**

D. The Balance Sheet
   1. Information is taken from
    a) Balance sheet columns of the work sheet.
    b) Ending balance from the statement of owner's equity.
   2. Types of balance sheets
    a) **Report form**
      (1) Liabilities and owner's equity are shown below the asset section.
      (2) Form used in this chapter.
    b) **Account form**
      (1) Assets are listed on the left.
      (2) Liability and owner's equity sections are listed on the right.

c) **Classified balance sheet**
    (1)   Similar items are grouped together.
    (2)   Balance sheet classifications
        (a)   **Current assets** include cash and items that will be converted into cash within the **operating cycle** of the business.
            (i)   Operating cycle is the period of time required to purchase supplies and services and convert them back into cash.
        (b)   **Property, plant, and equipment** include **plant** or **long-term assets** that are expected to serve the business for many years.
        (c)   **Current liabilities** include accounts payable, wages payable, and other items due within one year.
        (d)   **Long-term liabilities** include **long-term debts** such as mortgages payable that are not expected to be paid within a year.

In-Class Exercise: Complete Exercise 6-3A, 6-3B (15 minutes each)
In-Class Exercise: Complete Problem 6-6A, 6-6B (15 minutes each)

LO2

❖   **Transparency Master 6-4 illustrates Figure 6-4 The Closing Process.**

❖   **PowerPoint Slides 6-46 through 6-72 (generally) present the Closing Process**

II.   The **Closing Process (See Figure 6-4)**

Teaching Tip

➢   Closing means bringing the account to a zero balance. Each fiscal period is like a new ball game with a 0 starting score.

    A.   Accounts
        1.   **Permanent:** Assets, liabilities, and owner's equity are carried forward to each new accounting period.
        2.   **Temporary:** Revenue, expenses, and drawing accumulate information for a specific accounting period. At the end of the fiscal year, these accounts must be closed.

Teaching Tip

➢   Accounts reported on the balance sheet are permanent and remain open. All other accounts (those reported on the income statement and drawing) are temporary and closed.

        3.   **Income Summary** is a temporary owner's equity account used in the closing process to give accounts which are temporary a zero balance.

Teaching Tips

> The Income Summary is not really needed for the closing process. Some businesses simply close the revenue and expense accounts directly to the owner's capital account. One benefit of using the Income Summary account is that its balance before closing to the capital account equals the net income or net loss for the period. Thus, it can serve as a check of the accuracy of the closing entries for revenues and expenses.

> Some students may ask why Income Summary is not included with the other accounts on the work sheet. It is not included because it is not needed for the adjusting entries and is not used in the preparation of financial statements for a service business. Income Summary will be used later in the text for a merchandising business.

❖ **Transparency Master 6-6 illustrates Figure 6-6 Role of the Work Sheet in the Closing Process.**

❖ **Transparency Master 6-7 illustrates Figure 6-7 Closing Entries in T Account Form.**

    B.   Steps in the closing process **(See Figure 6-6 and Figure 6-7)**
        1.   Close revenue accounts to Income Summary.
            a)   Debit revenues.
            b)   Credit Income Summary.
        2.   Close expense accounts to Income Summary.
            a)   Debit Income Summary.
            b)   Credit expenses.

❖ **Transparency Master 6-5 illustrates Figure 6-5 Step 3: Closing Net Income and Closing Net Loss.**

        3.   Close Income Summary to Capital **(See Figure 6-5)**
            a)   Net Income
                (1)   Debit Income Summary.
                (2)   Credit Capital.
            b)   Net Loss
                (1)   Debit Capital.
                (2)   Credit Income Summary.
        4.   Close the Drawing to Capital
            a)   Debit Capital.
            b)   Credit Drawing.

Teaching Tip

> Students often want to treat drawing as an expense. Use this opportunity to reinforce the definition of an expense: a outflow of assets, or increase in liabilities, as a result of the efforts made to produce revenue. Withdrawals by the owner are not made in an attempt to produce revenue. Thus, withdrawals should not be treated in the same way as expenses.

❖ **PowerPoint Slides 6-54, 6-55, 6-61, 6-67 and 6-70 present Journalizing the Closing Entries**
III.   Journalize the Closing Entries **(See Figure 6-8)**

A. Journalize the closing entries on the year-end date.
B. Write "Closing Entries" in the Description column prior to making the first closing entry.
C. Explanations are not required in the Description column for individual closing entries.

❖ **PowerPoint Slides 6-71 and 6-72 present Posting the Closing Entries**

IV. Post the Closing Entries **(See Figure 6-9)**
   A. Post to the general ledger in the same manner as all other entries.
   B. Write "Closing" in the Item column of the general ledger.

LO3

❖ **PowerPoint Slides 6-73 and 6-74 present the Post-Closing Trial Balance**

V. **Post-Closing Trial Balance (See Figure 6-10)**
   A. Prepared to prove the equality of the debit and credit balances in the general ledger accounts.
   B. Only permanent accounts are included, since temporary accounts have been closed.

Teaching Tip

➢ All amounts reflected on the post-closing trial balance are the same as in the Balance Sheet columns of the work sheet except drawing and capital which are changed during the closing process.

In-Class Exercise: Complete Problem 6-8A, 6-8B (15 minutes each)

LO4

❖ **PowerPoint Slides 6-75 and 6-76 present the Accounting Cycle**

VI. The **Accounting Cycle**
   A. The steps involved in accounting for all of the business activities during an account period.
   B. Steps of the cycle are
      1. Analyze source documents.
      2. Journalize the transactions.
      3. Post to the ledger accounts.
      4. Prepare a trial balance.
      5. Determine and prepare the needed adjustments on the work sheet.
      6. Complete an end-of-period work sheet.
      7. Prepare an income statement, statement of owner's equity, and balance sheet.
      8. Journalize and post the adjusting entries.
      9. Journalize and post the closing entries.
      10. Prepare a post-closing trial balance.

Teaching Tips

> ➤ At the end of this chapter is a section called Computers and Accounting. This material introduces the student to the impact of computers on accounting systems.

> ➤ Following the end of this chapter is a comprehensive problem covering the accounting cycle.

Learning Activity

Using the accounts from your business, identify the current asset accounts; property, plant, and equipment accounts; and current liability accounts.

Critical Thinking Activity

Knowing how to classify accounts is a key piece of accounting knowledge. Reading a financial statement in today's business world is not limited to accounting personnel. Anyone involved with making business decisions must have a firm grasp of the parts of financial statements. By reviewing published financial statements, students can practice identifying the various classifications, such as current assets; current liabilities; and property, plant, and equipment.

Homework Suggestions

LO1 Study Guide Review Questions 1 through 13; Study Guide Exercises 1, 2; Study Guide Problems 4, 6; End of Chapter Questions 1, 2, 3, 4, 5; Exercise 6-1A, 6-1B.

LO2 Study Guide Review Questions 14 through 18; Study Guide Exercise 3; Study Guide Problems 5, 7, 8; End of Chapter Questions 6, 7, 8, 9; Exercises 6-4A, 6-4B, 6-5A, 6-5B.

LO3 Study Guide Review Question 19; Study Guide Problem 9; End of Chapter Question 10.

LO4 Study Guide Review Question 20; End of Chapter Question 11.

Entire Chapter:
Mastery Problem and Challenge Problem

Ten Questions Your Students Will Always Ask

1. How important is the placement of dollar signs and single and double lines?
2. Do you mean "the bottom line" is really two lines?
3. Should you always use "less" or "add" on financial statements, for instance, "add additional investments"?
4. Are accounts receivable always current assets?
5. Are computers, in today's world, current or long-term assets?
6. Would we treat a software license as short or long-term asset?

7. In other words, you do the opposite of the balance to close; i.e., if it has a debit balance—close with a credit?
8. So when you close an account, that amount goes into income summary?
9. If you close an account with a credit, then the debit is income summary?
10. Should the balance sheet and the post-closing trial balance have the same numbers?

Learning Objectives

LO1 Classify business transactions as operating, investing, or financing.
LO2 Prepare a statement of cash flows by analyzing and categorizing a series of business transactions.

LO1

Teaching Tip

➢ This appendix is intended to introduce the students to the purpose and format of the statement of cash flows. As you know, preparing the statement can get rather complicated. Here we introduce a very simple approach by using the cash T account. We do this so the student can get some hands-on work with the statement without unnecessary complexity at this point in the text. Later in the text, we will follow more traditional approaches.

❖ **PowerPoint Slides 6Apx-1 through 6Apx-5 present the Statement of Cash Flows and Operating, Investing and Financing Activities**

I. Statement of Cash Flows
    A. Explains what the business did to generate cash and how the cash was used.
    B. Categories of cash transactions
        1. **Operating activities**
            a) Related to the revenues and expenses reported on the Income Statement.
            b) Examples include cash received for services performed and cash paid for expenses.

Teaching Tip

➢ Interest income and interest expense are operating activities. Note that both appear on the income statement and are results of operating activities.

        2. **Investing activities**
            a) Purchasing and selling of long-term assets.
            b) Lending money.
            c) Collecting principal on related loans.
        3. **Financing activities**
            a) Transactions dealing with the exchange of cash between the business and its owners and creditors.
            b) Examples include owner's cash investments and cash withdrawals, borrowing money, and repaying the loan principal.

In-Class Exercise: Complete Exercise 6Apx-1A, 6Apx-1B (10 minutes each)

❖ Transparency Master 6-8 illustrates Figure 6A-1 Summary of Transactions for Jessica Jane's Campus Delivery.

❖ PowerPoint Slides 6Apx-6 through 6Apx-11 present Analysis of Transactions

II.   Summary of transactions **(See Figure 6A-1)**
    A.   Cash investment by owner
        1.   Financing activity.
        2.   Way to finance business and represents inflow from financing activity.
    B.   Purchased delivery equipment for cash
        1.   Investing activity.
        2.   Purchase of long-term assets is an investing activity.
    C.   Purchased delivery on account
        1.   No cash involved.
        2.   Does not affect Statement of Cash Flows.
    D.   Paid installment on delivery equipment
        1.   Financing activity.
        2.   Repayment of loan is financing activity.
    E.   Received cash for delivery services
        1.   Operating activity.
        2.   Cash received as result of operations is operating activity.
    F.   Paid rent
        1.   Operating activity.
        2.   Cash paid for expenses is an operating activity.
    G.   Paid telephone bill
        1.   Operating activity.
        2.   Cash paid for expenses is an operating activity.
    H.   Made deliveries on account
        1.   No cash involved.
        2.   Does not affect Statement of Cash Flows.
    I.   Purchased supplies for cash
        1.   Operating activity.
        2.   When supplies are used up, they become an expense.
        3.   Supplies are not long-term assets; therefore, this is not an investing activity.
    J.   Paid cash for insurance policy.
        1.   Operating activity.
        2.   When insurance is used, it becomes an expense.
        3.   Prepaid Insurance is not a long-term asset.
    K.   Received cash on account
        1.   Operating activity.
        2.   Cash received as a result of providing services.
    L.   Purchased delivery equipment. Made down payment. Put the rest on account.
        1.   Investing activity.
        2.   Purchase of long-term assets are investing activity.
        3.   Only the down payment will be recorded on the Statement of Cash Flows.
    M.   Paid wages
        1.   Operating activity.
        2.   Payment of expenses is an operating activity.
    N.   Earned delivery fees in cash and on account
        1.   Operating activity.
        2.   Cash received as a result of operations is operating activity.

3.   Only the fees received in cash will be recorded on the Statement of Cash Flows.

O.   Owner withdrawal
1.   Financing activity.
2.   Payments to owners are part of the financing activities of a business.

LO2

❖   **Transparency Master 6-10 illustrates Figure 6A-3 Statement of Cash Flows for Jessica Jane's Campus Delivery.**

❖   **PowerPoint Slides 6Apx-12 through 6Apx-19 present the Statement of Cash Flows**

III.   Preparing the Statement of Cash Flows **(See Figure 6A-3)**

❖   **Transparency Master 6-9 illustrates Figure 6A-2 Cash T Account for Jessica Jane's Campus Delivery with Classifications of Cash Transactions.**

A.   Summarize the cash transactions on a T account. **(See Figure 6A-2)**
B.   Use this summary to prepare the Statement of Cash Flows.
C.   Heading
1.   Name of company.
2.   Name of statement.
3.   Time period for which statement is prepared.
D.   Three main body sections
1.   Cash Flows from Operating Activities
   a)   List cash received from customers.
   b)   List cash paid for operating activities.
   c)   Subtract to find net cash paid or provided by operating activities.
2.   Cash Flows from Investing Activities
   a)   List cash paid for long-term assets.
   b)   List cash received from the sale or disposal of long-term assets.
   c)   Subtract to find net cash paid or provided by investing activities.
3.   Cash Flows from Financing Activities
   a)   List cash invested by owner.
   b)   List cash withdrawn by owner.
   c)   List principal payments made on loans.
   d)   Subtract to find net cash paid or provided by financing activities.
E.   Totaling the Statement of Cash Flows
1.   Add and/or subtract the inflows and outflows.
2.   This total is labeled as net increase (decrease) in cash and should equal the net increase (decrease) reported in the cash account during the period.

In-Class Exercise: Complete Problem 6Apx-2A. Problem 6Apx-2B (25 minutes each)

Learning Activity

Ask the students to think of different types of business transactions. As they offer examples, ask them to classify the transaction. With a little persuasion, the terms operating, investing, and financing seem quite natural. Ask them to try to think of a transaction that does not fit into one of the categories. If they do, let us (Jim Heintz or Rob Parry) know. We don't think that there are any. By breaking all business activities into three basic classifications, the concept of running a business is simplified. Helping your students to classify transactions in this way will help them learn about the statement of cash flows and business in general.

Homework Suggestions

LO1 Study Guide Apx. Exercises 1, 2; Study Guide Problem 3; End of Appendix Question 1.

LO2 Study Guide Problem 4; End of Appendix Question 2.

Learning Objectives

LO1 Describe how to open and use a checking account.
LO2 Prepare a bank reconciliation and related journal entries.
LO3 Establish and use a petty cash fund.
LO4 Establish a change fund and use the cash short and over account.

LO1

❖ **PowerPoint Slides 7-1 through 7-3 present Accounting for Cash**

I. Accounting for Cash
    A. **Cash** includes currency, coins, checks, money orders, and cashier's checks.
    B. Because cash plays such a central role in operating a business, a system of **internal control** is necessary.

Teaching Tip

➤ Emphasize that all businesses—large and small—need an internal control system. Such a system protects all assets, not just cash, and ensures that the accounting records are correct.

    C. A checking account is used to protect and properly manage cash.
    D. Deposit slips and monthly bank statements verify cash received.
    E. Cancelled checks and bank statements verify cash payments.

❖ **PowerPoint Slides 7-4 through 7-11 present Checking Accounts**

II. Checking Account

Teaching Tips

➤ Consider visiting a bank or having a bank representative come to your class to discuss opening a checking account, using an ATM, and other bank services. At a minimum, ask a student who recently opened a checking account to describe the process.

➤ Bring to class or have students bring to class examples of deposit tickets, checks and stubs, endorsed checks, ATM cards, and bank statements. This both brings to life the material and shows the many types of these items.

    A. Opening a checking account
        1. **Signature card** must be completed and signed by an authorized person. **(See Figure 7-1)**
        2. Depositor's social security number or employer identification number is shown on the card to identify the depositor.

B.   Making deposits

❖   **Transparency Master 7-1 illustrates Figure 7-2 Deposit Ticket.**

              1.   **Deposit ticket** is a detailed listing of the items being deposited. **(See Figure 7-2)**

              2.   Checks are identified by their **ABA (American Bankers Association) numbers**.

Teaching Tip

➤   Point out that depositors often do not list ABA numbers on deposit slips. Banks still accept deposits.

              3.   **Endorsements**

Teaching Tip

➤   Point out that the law now requires endorsements to be placed at the top 1 1/2 inches of the left side of the back of the check. Lines often are provided for the endorsement.

                  a)   **Blank endorsement** is payable to any bearer.

❖   **Transparency Master 7-2 illustrates Figure 7-3 Restrictive Endorsement.**

                  b)   **Restrictive endorsement** is payable to a specific bank or person. **(See Figure 7-3)**

              4.   **Automated Teller Machines (ATMs)** allow depositors to make deposits or withdrawals at all times.

                  a)   Each depositor has a plastic card. **(See Figure 7-4)**

                  b)   Each depositor has a personal identification number (PIN).

C.   Writing checks

Teaching Tip

➤   Emphasize that no part of a check should ever be written in pencil.

              1.   Three parties to each check

                  a)   **Drawer** orders the bank to pay the cash.

                  b)   **Drawee** is the bank on which the check is drawn.

                   c)   **Payee** is the person being paid the cash.

              2.   Recording supplies

❖   **Transparency Master 7-3 illustrates Figure 7-5 Checks and Check Stubs.**

                  a)   **Check stubs (See Figure 7-5)**

                  b)   Check register

                  c)   Software packages

              3.   Steps in preparing a **check**

                  a)   Complete the check stub or register.

       b)   Enter the date, payee name, and the amount of the check.

       c)   Sign the check.

❖   **Transparency Master 7-4 illustrates Figure 7-6 Bank Statement.**

    D.   **Bank Statement (See Figure 7-6)**
       1.   Gives the balance at the beginning of the period.
       2.   Lists deposits and other amounts added during the period.
       3.   Lists checks and other amounts subtracted during the period.
       4.   Gives the balance at the end of the period.
       5.   Provides the depositor with **cancelled** checks and other documentation.

In-Class Exercise: Complete Exercise 7-1A, 7-2A, 7-3A, 7-1B, 7-2B, and 7-3B (5 minutes each)

LO2

❖   **PowerPoint Slides 7-12 through 7-41 present Reconciling the Bank Statement**

III.   Reconciling the Bank Statement

Teaching Tip

➤   Note that a bank reconciliation is important to identify not only your errors but also the bank's. Bank records are not perfect either.

❖   **Transparency Master 7-5 illustrates Figure 7-7 Depositor and Bank Records—Deposits.**

    A.   Deposits **(See Figure 7-7)**

❖   **Transparency Master 7-6 illustrates Figure 7-8 Depositor and Bank Records—Cash Payments.**

    B.   Cash payments **(See Figure 7-8)**
    C.   Reasons for differences between bank and book balances
       1.   Outstanding checks
       2.   Deposits in transit
       3.   **Service charges**
       4.   Collections
       5.   **Not sufficient fund (NSF)** checks

Teaching Tip

➤   Ask a student to explain what happens when a check they received and deposited in their account is not honored by the check writer's bank. It is likely that some students have experienced this.

       6.   Errors
    D.   Steps in preparing the **bank reconciliation**

Teaching Tip

➢ Explain to students that when reconciling they are to first put on a banker's "hat"— think like a banker—and account for all the bank has no knowledge of. Then, they are to put on the business' "hat"— think like the business— and account for all the business has no knowledge of.

    1. Identify deposits in transit and any related errors.
       a) Deposits in transit from last month's bank reconciliation should be listed on current month's bank statement.
       b) Deposits listed in accounting records but not on the bank statement are **deposits in transit** on the current bank reconciliation.
       c) Deposit amounts on the bank statement should match the accounting records.
    2. Identify **outstanding checks** and related errors.
       a) **Cancelled checks** from last month's bank reconciliation should be listed on the current month's bank statement.
       b) Check off checks from the bank statement that have cleared.
       c) Checks written but not checked off are outstanding.
    3. Identify additional reconciling items.

Teaching Tip

➢ A depositor's account is a liability to the bank. Thus, a credit memo increases this liability; a debit memo reduces the liability.

       a) Check for **credit memos.**
       b) Check for **debit memos.**

Teaching Tip

➢ Recall from Chapter 4 that transposition errors can be identified because they are evenly divisible by nine.

In-Class Exercise: Complete Exercise 7-4A, 7-4B (10 minutes each)
In-Class Exercise: Complete Problem 7-8A, 7-8B (5 minutes each)

❖ **Transparency Master 7-7 illustrates Figure 7-9 Bank Reconciliation Format.**

❖ **Transparency Master 7-8 illustrates Figure 7-10 Bank Reconciliation.**

    E. Illustration of a bank reconciliation **(See Figure 7-9 and Figure 7-10)**

Teaching Tip

> Call attention to the fact that items in the lower half of the bank reconciliation, where the *adjusted bank balance* is computed, always require journal entries.

❖ **PowerPoint Slides 7-42 through 7-51 present Journal Entries**

    F.   Journal entries **(See Figure 7-11)**
        1.   Errors in the books.
        2.   Bank additions and deductions that do not already appear in the accounting records.

In-Class Exercise: Complete Exercise 7-5A, 7-5B (10 minutes each)

    G.   **Electronic funds transfer (EFT)** uses a computer rather than paper checks to complete bank transactions.

Teaching Tip

> Note that another type of EFT (Electronic Funds Transfer) is used by bank customers to pay utility bills and make mortgage payments without checks.

LO3

❖ **PowerPoint Slides 7-52 through 7-62 present Petty Cash**

IV.   The Petty Cash Fund
    A.   Establishing a **petty cash fund**
        1.   A check is written to a custodian for the amount of the fund.
        2.   The custodian should be the only person authorized to make payments from the fund.
    B.   Making payments from the petty cash fund
        1.   **Petty cash vouchers** are prepared for each payment. **(See Figure 7-12)**
        2.   Vouchers should be signed by the custodian and the person receiving the cash.
        3.   Vouchers should be numbered consecutively.

Teaching Tips

> It is important to emphasize that the Petty Cash Payments Record is **not a journal**. This will help students to understand the journal entry made to replenish the petty cash fund.

> Note that each payment is entered twice in the Petty Cash Payments Record–once in the Total Amount column and once in the Distribution of Payments columns.

❖   **Transparency Master 7-9 illustrates Figure 7-13 Maple Consulting's Petty Cash Payments Record.**

        C.   **Petty cash payments record (See Figure 7-13)**
            1.   Multicolumn record that supplements the regular accounting records.
            2.   Petty cash payments record is not a journal.
        D.   Replenishing the petty cash fund

Teaching Tip

➤   Some students invariably want to debit Petty Cash when the fund is replenished. A way to convince them to debit the expense accounts is to remind them that the Petty Cash Payments Record is **not a journal.** No expenses have been recorded and the Petty Cash account still has the same balance as when it was established. Therefore, the journal entry must debit the expenses and credit Cash, which gets consumed as the petty cash payments are made.

            1.   Replenished when the fund runs low.
            2.   Replenished at the end of an accounting period.
            3.   Information in the petty cash payments record is used to replenish the petty cash fund.

In-Class Exercise: Complete Exercise 7-6A, 7-6B (10 minutes each)

LO4

Teaching Tips

➤   When comparing cash in the register and the register tape, remember to include the change fund.

➤   Tell students that Cash Short and Over can be treated as an expense account in the chart of accounts. Shortages (expenses) are more common than overages because customers are less likely to complain about receiving too much change.

❖   **PowerPoint Slides 7-63 through 7-75 present Change Fund and Cash Short and Over**

V.   Change Fund and Cash Short and Over
        A.   Establish a change fund
        B.   Cash short and over
            1.   Account is used when errors in cash are made.
            2.   Debited when cash is short.
            3.   Credited when cash is over.

In-Class Exercise: Complete Exercise 7-7A, 7-7B (10 minutes each)
In-Class Exercise: Complete Problem 7-11A, 7-11B (10 minutes each)

1. Have the students compare their personal checks with those of other students in the class. Identify the ABA numbers.

2. Ask the students to share their companies' cash short and over policies.

3. Ask the students to share their on-the-job experiences with petty cash.

4. This exercise is to help students understand the petty cash fund. Establish a petty cash custodian "volunteer." Provide this individual with a large black box labeled Petty Cash. Tell the custodian the amount of the fund but actually shortchange it by several hundred dollars. (Students do not usually think to count the money first). Next, several student salespersons request advances or reimbursements. Upon dispensing funds, the custodian writes the reason on an index card. Soon, provide a surprise audit. The custodian will be quite surprised at the shortage. Students are very good at discovering for themselves the problems of the system, which is far more important than journal entries to set up and replenish the fund. Discuss the opportunities for mistakes and dishonesty in the system.**

** Marianne Fox, "Internal Controls," *Great Ideas in Teaching Introductory Accounting,* South-Western College Publishing, Cincinnati, Ohio, 1996, p. 45

Critical Thinking Activity

Have the students prepare a written bank reconciliation for their own personal checking accounts following the formatting guidelines presented in the text.

Homework Suggestions

LO1 Study Guide Review Questions 1 through 14; Study Guide Exercises 1, 2; End of Chapter Questions 1, 2, 3, 4

LO2 Study Guide Review Questions 15 through 20; Study Guide Exercises 3, 4; Study Guide Problem 7; End of Chapter Questions 5, 6, 7, 8; Problem 7-9A, 7-9B

LO3 Study Guide Review Questions 21 through 24; Study Guide Exercise 5; Study Guide Problem 8; End of Chapter Questions 9, 10, 11, 12; Problem 7-10A, 7-10B

LO4 Study Guide Review Questions 25 through 27; Study Guide Exercise 6; Study Guide Problem 9; End of Chapter Questions 13, 14

Entire Chapter:
Mastery Problem and Challenge Problem.

Ten Questions Your Students Will Always Ask

1. Do banks really compare signature card signatures to check signatures?
2. Do businesses really use the ABA number of their customers' checks when making a deposit?
3. Are businesses able to deposit checks not made out exactly like their business name?
4. What happens when a night deposit is lost by the bank?

5. Can a stamp be a signature?
6. How often is the bank really incorrect?
7. How do you prove the bank is incorrect?
8. Where does journalizing the bank reconciliation fall with respect to other end-of-period journalizing activities?
9. How small or large should the petty cash fund be?
10. Is Cash Short and Over used when petty cash is short or over?

Learning Objectives

LO1 Distinguish between employees and independent contractors
LO2 Calculate employee earnings and deductions
LO3 Describe and prepare payroll records
LO4 Account for employee earnings and deductions
LO5 Describe various payroll record-keeping methods

Teaching Tip

➢ Begin coverage of this chapter by admitting to students that we deliberately kept things simple in prior chapters by debiting Wages Expense and crediting Cash for employee wages. As this chapter shows, the real accounting for employee payroll is much more complicated.

LO1

❖ **PowerPoint 8-1 through 8-7 present Payroll Record Keeping and Employees and Independent Contractors**

I.   Employees and Independent Contractors
    A.   Distinction
        1.   **Employees**
            a)   Employee works under the control of an employer.
            b)   Employer must maintain detailed records of employment.
        2.   **Independent contractors**
            a)   Perform services for a fee.
            b)   Are not controlled by the company paying the fee.
            c)   Company does not need to maintain detailed records.

Teaching Tip

➢ Ask students to provide additional examples of employees and independent contractors. How would students classify a college professor?

    B.   Forms filed
        1.   Employer prepares Form W-2 for the employee.
        2.   Company sends Form 1099 to the independent contractor.

LO2

❖ **PowerPoint 8-8 through 8-38 present Employee Earnings and Deductions**

II.   Employee Earnings and Deductions

Teaching Tip

➤ As an incentive for students to learn the sometimes tedious payroll procedures, remind them that every accountant must know how to account for payroll. Also, many other jobs require knowledge of payroll and what its numbers mean. Thus, if they want a job, they need to know payroll.

    A. Salaries and Wages
        1. Compute earnings.
        2. Determine deductions.
        3. **Salaries** are paid weekly, biweekly, semimonthly, or monthly.

Teaching Tip

➤ There are 52 weeks in each year but not 4 weeks in each month. That is why salaries must be annualized before determining the hourly rate.

        4. **Wages** are paid based on a rate per hour or units produced.

Teaching Tips

➤ Have students find out what the current minimum wage is. Also have them report what the amounts have been during the past ten years.

➤ It may be interesting to show some fairly complex units of production payment methods and ask your students if they know of any others.

    B. Computing total earnings
        1. Salaries are usually the same from one payment period to another.
        2. Time cards are kept to compute employee wages. **(See Figure 8-1 and Figure 8-2)**
        3. Employees covered under the **Fair Labor Standards Act** must be paid overtime at 1.5 times the employee's hourly rate when an employee works more than forty hours in a week.
    C. Deductions from total earnings
        1. **Gross pay** - deductions = **net pay**.
        2. Employees have income tax withheld for federal, state, and local governments.
        3. **Withholding allowances** reduce the amounts withheld from an employee's pay. **(See Figure 8-3)**
        4. Employee's federal income tax withholding
            a) Employers generally use **wage-bracket method**.
            b) Wage-bracket tables provided by IRS in *Circular E - Employer's Tax Guide* **(See Figure 8-4)**

Teaching Tip

➢ Bring copies of the various payroll forms and *Circular E* to class. Have students obtain a copy of *Circular E* from the local IRS office or from the Internet. Payroll is a constantly changing area, and students can compare the requirements in the most current *Circular E* with those in the text.

     c) Four factors determine amount withheld
        (1) total earnings
        (2) marital status
        (3) number of withholding allowances claimed
        (4) length of pay period

Teaching Tips

➢ Walk through several examples of weekly earnings and withholding allowances so students can see how to use the tables.

➢ If your state or city has an income tax, describe how the withholding is handled.

     5. Employee **FICA tax** withholding
        a) Social Security taxes provide pension and disability benefits.
        b) Medicare taxes provide health insurance.

Teaching Tips

➢ Note that according to current rules, the Social Security tax of 6.2% stops after $76,200, but that all earnings are subject to the Medicare tax of 1.45%. When the Social Security program was established in 1937, the tax was 1% on earnings up to $3,000 per year!

➢ Calculations of various payroll taxes often require rounding of dollar amounts. Depending on the level and background of your students, you might want to review rounding rules at this point.

     6. Voluntary deductions can be withheld from the employee's pay at the discretion of the employee.

In-Class Exercise: Complete Exercise 8-1A, 8-1B (10 minutes each)
In-Class Exercise: Complete Exercise 8-2A, 8-2B (5 minutes each)
In-Class Exercise: Complete Exercise 8-3A, 8-3B (10 minutes each)
In-Class Exercise: Complete Exercise 8-4A, 8-4B (5 minutes each)
In-Class Exercise: Complete Exercise 8-5A, 8-5B (10 minutes each)
In-Class Exercise: Complete Problem 8-8A, 8-8B (10 minutes each)

LO3

❖   **PowerPoint 8-39 through 8-85 present Payroll Records**

III.   Payroll Records

❖   **Transparency Master 8-1 illustrates Figure 8-5 Payroll Register (left and right sides)**

     A.   **Payroll register (See Figure 8-5)**
        1.   Multi-column form used to compute data every payroll period.
        2.   Information is taken from time cards and pay rates.

Teaching Tips

➤   Walk through the payroll register to clarify the meaning and source of the information in each column. Have students verify the withholding amounts for several of the employees by using the withholding tax tables.

➤   For some reason, some students have great difficulty with the idea of taxable earnings so several walk-throughs or, if time permits, their individual responses would be very helpful.

     B.   Payroll check **(See Figure 8-6)**
        1.   Methods of payment
            a)   Cash
            b)   Check
            c)   **Direct deposit**
        2.   The amount of the check is taken from the net pay column of the payroll register.

❖   **Transparency Master 8-2 illustrates Figure 8-7 Employee Earnings Record (left and right sides)**

     C.   **Employee earnings record (See Figure 8-7)**
        1.   Separate records are kept for each employee.
        2.   Information is obtained from the payroll register.

Teaching Tip

➤   Have students verify that the amounts entered in Istone's employee earnings record for 12/19 (Figure 8-7) are the same as in the payroll register in Figure 8-5.

LO4

❖   **Transparency Master 8-3 illustrates Figure 8-8 Accounting for Payroll**

❖   **PowerPoint 8-86 through 8-98 present Accounting for Employee Earnings and Deductions**

IV.   Accounting for Employee Earnings and Deductions **(See Figure 8-8)**
     A.   Journalizing payroll transactions
        1.   Totals from the payroll register provide the data for journalizing the employee's payroll information.

2. Salary and Wages Expense is debited for the gross pay.
3. Deductions from wages (which are liabilities) are credited along with cash (which is net pay).
   B. Wages and Salaries Expense
     1. Account is debited for the gross pay for each pay period.
     2. Separate accounts may be used for salaries and wages.
   C. Employee Income Tax Payable
     1. Account is credited for the amounts withheld.
     2. Account is debited when the tax is paid.

Teaching Tip

➢ Have students trace each amount from the journal entry to the column totals in the payroll register in Figure 8-5. Students might notice that "Federal Income Tax" from the payroll register becomes "Employee Income Tax Payable" in the journal entry. Explain that this account title is needed to distinguish this income tax from the federal income tax imposed on a business as a corporation (Chapter 23).

   D. Social Security and Medicare Taxes Payable
     1. Accounts are credited for the amounts withheld and for the employer's portion as well.
     2. FICA taxes and Employee Income Tax Payable are paid to the IRS.
   E. Other deductions
     1. Voluntary deductions are credited when deducted from the employee's pay.
     2. Health insurance and United Way are two common deductions.

In-Class Exercise: Complete Exercise 8-6A, 8-6B (10 minutes each)
In-Class Exercise: Complete Exercise 8-7A, 8-7B (10 minutes each)
In-Class Exercise: Complete Problem 8-9A, 8-9B (5 minutes each)
In-Class Exercise: Complete Problem 8-10A, 8-10B (10 minutes each)

LO5

❖ **PowerPoint 8-99 through 8-101 present Payroll Record Keeping Methods**

V. Payroll Record-Keeping Methods
   A. **Manual System**
     1. All records are prepared by hand.
     2. Information is recorded in several places.
       a) Payroll register
       b) Paycheck and stub
       c) Employees earnings record
     3. If an employer has many employees, this system can be inefficient and costly.
   B. **Payroll processing center**
     1. Business that sells payroll record keeping services.
     2. Employer provides the center with all basic employee data and each period's report of hours worked.

3.   Processing center maintains all payroll records and prepares each period's payroll checks.
4.   Fees are cost efficient.

❖   **Transparency Master 8-4 illustrates Figure 8-9 Electronic Payroll System**

C.   **Electronic system (See Figure 8-9)**
1.   Computer system based on a software package that performs all payroll record keeping and prepares payroll checks.
2.   Only the employee number and hours worked need to be entered into the computer each pay period.
3.   Computer calculates
a)   Gross pay
b)   Deductions
c)   Net pay
4.   Outputs
a)   Payroll register
b)   Checks
c)   Employees earnings record

Teaching Tips

➢   Note that payroll typically is one of the first accounting functions to be computerized by businesses.

➢   Have students interview a payroll manager, a manager of a payroll service center, or an office manager of a small office who handles payroll. Ask how the payroll system works, what type of system is used, and how computers are used in processing payroll.

Learning Activities

1.   Students can be motivated to take an interest in FICA taxes by encouraging them to check on the status of their own accounts. Have them call the Social Security Administration to request a form for this purpose.

2.   Have the students bring in one of their own paycheck stubs. From these stubs, have them journalize the payroll entry for that payroll period. Also, have the students determine if FUTA and SUTA are to be declared. If they are, have the students record the journal entry for payroll taxes for the payroll period.

Critical Thinking Activities

1.   Have a discussion in class, or have the students write a report on the ramifications of hiring employees versus independent contractors. The students could be asked to set up the required payroll record keeping systems for both situations. The students should be aware of the regulations that apply to the hiring of employees and independent contractors. The instructor should note that the IRS is investigating businesses that have hired independent contractors who are in fact and by law employees. The IRS can exact severe penalties on businesses that violate the law.

64

2. Divide the students into groups of three or four. Assign the groups one of the three common methods of payroll processing: manual, electronic, or payroll processing centers. Ask each group to prepare a presentation (or written report). Groups should analyze the following:

   1. When is this method most cost efficient?
   2. What knowledge of tax laws is needed by the employer?
   3. What information must be determined each payroll period?
   4. What procedures are used each payroll period to prepare the payroll?
   5. Other information.

   Select groups to present their findings to the class.

Homework Suggestions

LO1 Study Guide Review Questions 1, 2; End of Chapter Question 1.
LO2 Study Guide Review Questions 3 through 12; Study Guide Exercises 1, 2, 3; End of Chapter Questions 2, 3, 4.
LO3 Study Guide Review Questions 13, 14, 15; Study Guide Problem 7; End of Chapter Questions 5, 6, 7.
LO4 Study Guide Exercises 4, 5; Study Guide Problem 6; End of Chapter Questions 8, 9.
LO5 Study Guide Review Question 16; End of Chapter Question 10.
Entire Chapter:
   Mastery Problem and Challenge Problem.

Ten Questions Your Students Will Always Ask

1. Can anyone be considered an independent contractor, or is there some standard to go by in determining whether a person is an employee or an independent contractor?
2. Are salaried employees sometimes paid overtime; if so, how is their pay determined?
3. So, if you make a lot of money, you don't have to pay Social Security taxes anymore?
4. Now, the only numbers to go in the cumulative earnings column are "all" the money earned this year?
5. Is there ever a cumulative earnings column before the current earnings column?
6. Do all of this pay period's earnings go into taxable earnings?
7. In other words, taxable earnings will sometimes be blank?
8. So what the employer deducts or takes from the employees' checks is a liability of the employer?
9. How long are employee payroll records kept?
10. If a computer can and does do all this, why do we have to learn the manual methods in such detail?

Learning Objectives

LO1   Describe and calculate employer payroll taxes
LO2   Account for employer payroll taxes expense
LO3   Describe employer reporting and payment responsibilities
LO4   Describe and account for workers' compensation insurance

LO1

❖   **PowerPoint Slides 9-1 through 9-16 present Employer Payroll Taxes**

I.   Employer Payroll Taxes
   A.   **Employer's FICA tax**
      1.   Employer pays at the same rate and same earnings bases as the employee.

Teaching Tip

➢   Emphasize that <u>both</u> the employer and employee are subjected to Social Security and Medicare taxes. Half of the total tax for these programs is paid by the employee. The other half is levied directly on the employer.

❖   **Transparency Master 9-1 illustrates Figure 9-1 Payroll Register (left and right sides)**

      2.   Payroll register provides the information necessary to compute employer payroll taxes. **(See Figure 9-1) (See also Figure 8-5)**

Teaching Tip

➢   Have students compare the payroll register in Figure 9-1 with the one in Figure 8-5 in Chapter 8, so they remember the source of this information.

   B.   Self-employment tax
      1.   Individuals who own and run their own business are considered self-employed.
      2.   **Self-employment income** is the net income of a trade or business run by an individual.
      3.   Business owners pay FICA tax on their net income if it is $400 or more.
      4.   **Self-employment tax** is a contribution to the FICA tax program.

Teaching Tip

➢   Explain the logic for the self-employment tax rate being approximately double the employer and employee Social Security and Medicare rates. The self-employed person is considered both the employer and employee.

❖   **Transparency Master 9-2 illustrates Figure 9-2 Computation of FUTA Tax**

C. Employer's **FUTA (Federal Unemployment Tax Act) tax (See Figure 9-2)**
  1. Purpose is to raise funds to administer the combined federal/state unemployment program.
  2. Federal rate is commonly .8% of the first $7,000 of earnings for each employee.

Teaching Tips

➢ Note that the effective FUTA rate cannot be less than .8%, **even if the state rate exceeds 5.4%.**

➢ Point out that if the employer qualifies for a lower state rate for merit reasons, the employer still would receive full credit up to 5.4% in computing the FUTA tax.

❖ **Transparency Master 9-3 illustrates Figure 9-3 Computation of SUTA Tax**

D. Employer's **SUTA (State Unemployment Tax) tax (See Figure 9-3)**
  1. Purpose is to raise funds to pay unemployment benefits.
  2. Tax rates, earnings bases, and unemployment benefits vary among the states.
  3. **Merit-rating system** is used in most states to encourage employers to provide stable employment to workers.

Teaching Tips

➢ Bring your state's unemployment tax form to class for illustration. These forms vary across the states. Note that in a few states, employees must pay state unemployment tax.

➢ Have students interview personnel at the local unemployment office about how and when unemployment may be collected.

LO2

❖ **Transparency Master 9-4 illustrates Figure 9-4 Accounting for Payroll Taxes**
❖ **PowerPoint Slides 9-17 through 9-25 present the same information**

II. Accounting for Employer Payroll Taxes **(See Figure 9-4)**
  A. Journalizing employer payroll taxes
    1. Obtain the taxable earnings amounts from the Taxable Earnings column of the payroll register.

Teaching Tip

➢ It may be necessary to walk through once again how taxable earnings are determined.

  2. Compute the amount of the employer FICA tax.
  3. Compute the amount of Medicare tax.
  4. Compute the amount of FUTA tax.

        5.   Compute the amount of SUTA tax.

        6.   Prepare the journal entry using the amounts computed in steps 2-5.

    B.   Payroll Taxes Expense is the account used for debiting all the employer payroll taxes.

Teaching Tips

➢   Explain that the reason we credit separate liability accounts is that some of the taxes are paid at different times to different taxing authorities.

➢   Now would be a good time to reinforce the idea that both Chapters 8 and 9 cover payroll—that payroll is in two parts—employees (wages and salaries expense) and employers (payroll tax expense).

    C.   Social Security and Medicare Taxes Payable

        1.   Accounts are credited to enter the amount of the Social Security and Medicare taxes imposed on the employer.

        2.   Accounts are debited when the tax is paid.

Teaching Tip

➢   Point out that there is no need for separate liability accounts for employer and employee Social Security and Medicare taxes payable. Both the employer and employee taxes are due and will be paid to the IRS.

    D.   FUTA Tax Payable

        1.   Account credited for the tax imposed on the employer.

        2.   Account is debited when the tax is paid.

    E.   SUTA Tax Payable

        1.   Account credited for the tax imposed on employers to fund state unemployment benefits.

        3.   Account is debited when the tax is paid.

❖   **PowerPoint Slides 9-26 through 9-31 present Total Costs of an Employee**

    F.   Total payroll costs

        1.   Gross wages

        2.   Employer FICA and Medicare tax

        3.   SUTA tax

        4.   FUTA tax

Teaching Tip

➢   The issue of the total cost of employing a person is one that most students have never considered. It is interesting to bring up medical insurance, pension plans, paid vacations, and other fringe costs as well.

In-Class Exercise: Complete Exercise 9-2A, 9-2B (15 minutes each)

In-Class Exercise: Complete Exercise 9-3A, 9-3B (15 minutes each)

In-Class Exercise: Complete Exercise 9-4A, 9-4B (10 minutes each)

LO3

❖ **PowerPoint Slides 9-32 through 9-49 present Reporting and Payment Responsibilities**

III.   Reporting and Payment Responsibilities **(See Figure 9-11)**
       A.   Federal income tax withholding and Social Security and Medicare taxes.

❖ **Transparency Master 9-5 illustrates Figure 9-5 Summary of Deposit Rules**

    1. Determining when payments are due according to the deposit rules stated in *Circular E-Employer's Tax Guide.* **(See Figure 9-5)**

Teaching Tip

➢   As in Chapter 8, *Circular E* is a key source of payroll accounting information. Students should be using a current copy of *Circular E* to follow along with and update the text, as needed. Have teams of students gather all the forms needed for federal payroll tax reporting. Use the forms to prepare a timeline showing when the various forms must be filed and deposits made.

❖   **Transparency Master 9-6 illustrates Figure 9-6 Federal Tax Deposit Coupon (Form 8109)**

    2.   Use of Form 8109, Federal Tax Deposit Coupon **(See Figure 9-6)**
       a)   Deposits are made at an authorized bank using Form 8109.
       b)   **Employer Identification Number (EIN)** must be on the Form 8109.
       c)   Amount of tax paid is debited to the tax accounts and Cash is credited.

❖   **Transparency Master 9-7 illustrates Figure 9-7 Employer's Quarterly Federal Tax Return (Form 941)**

    3.   Form 941 **(See Figure 9-7)**
       a)   Filed with the IRS at the end of the month following each calendar quarter.
       b)   Reports the employee federal income tax and Social Security and Medicare tax withholding.
       c)   Reports employer Social Security and Medicare taxes for the quarter.

In-Class Exercise: Complete Exercise 9-5A, 9-5B (10 minutes each)

❖   **Transparency Master 9-8 illustrates Figure 9-8 Employer's Annual Federal Unemployment (FUTA) Tax Return (Form 940)**

    B.   FUTA Taxes **(See Figure 9-8)**
       1.   FUTA taxes must be paid using Form 8109 when the accumulated liability exceeds $100.
       2.   Debit FUTA Tax Payable and credit Cash.
       3.   Form 940 is used to report FUTA wages and taxes following the end of the calendar year.

C.   SUTA Taxes
       1.   Taxes are usually reported and paid on a quarterly basis.
       2.   Debit SUTA Tax Payable and credit Cash.

❖   **Transparency Master 9-9 illustrates Figure 9-9 Wage and Tax Statement (Form W-2)**

D.   Employee wage and tax statement - Form W-2 **(See Figure 9-9)**
       1.   Information is taken from the employee earnings records.
       2.   Required to be furnished to employees by January 31.
       3.   Form W-2 copies are needed for the following
           a)   Copy A - sent to the Social Security Administration
           b)   Copy B - employee attaches to federal income tax return
           c)   Copy C - employee keeps for personal records
           d)   Copy D - employer retains for company records
           e)   Copy 1 - employer sends to state or local income tax department
           f)   Copy 2 - employee attaches to state or local income tax return

Teaching Tip

➢   Point out that the number of copies needed for Form W-2 will vary, depending on whether there are state and city income taxes. Ask students how many copies of the W-2 they received from their employers.

❖   **Transparency Master 9-10 illustrates Figure 9-10 Transmittal of Wage and Tax Statements (Form W-3)**

E.   Summary of employee wages and taxes **(See Figure 9-10)**

Teaching Tip

➢   Note that the complexity of payroll reports, deposit rules, and due dates is a major reason small businesses often hire an accountant to handle payroll.

F.   Summary of reports and payments **(See Figure 9-11)**

Teaching Tip

➢   The reporting and payment of employee and employer taxes is a very important obligation of every employer. The students should be aware that payroll tax reporting is very important to all sectors of employment. Companies must hire competent people to make sure all of their payroll taxes are reported and paid on time. Very severe penalties can be assessed on an employer who does not report on a timely basis. Accountants should discuss with businesses that are thinking of hiring employees the duties and filing responsibilities that every employer must perform.

LO4

❖   **PowerPoint Slides 9-50 through 9-56 present Workers' Compensation Insurance**

IV.   **Workers' Compensation Insurance**
    A.   Required by most states that employers carry this insurance.

Teaching Tip

➢   Describe your state's workers' compensation program for the students. Note that in a limited number of states (possibly yours), the employees are required to contribute to this program.

    B.   Provides insurance for employees who suffer job-related injuries.
    C.   Cost of insurance
        1.   Usually paid by the employer
        2.   Depends on the following
            a)   Number of employees
            b)   Riskiness of the job
            c)   Company's accident history
    D.   Time and amount of payment will vary with state.

Teaching Tip

➢   Refer students to the Computers and Accounting coverage in this chapter. This will help them understand how computers are assisting in accounting for payroll-related transactions.

In-Class Exercise: Complete Exercise 9-6A, 9-6B (10 minutes each)
In-Class Exercise: Complete Problem 9-9A, 9-9B (15 minutes each

Learning Activities

1.   Chapter 9 is about the reporting and payment of payroll taxes. Often people think workers' compensation is a payroll tax. It is insurance that is reported and paid depending upon the circumstances listed above. Workers' compensation insurance can be a huge cost to any employer. Students and employers should be aware there are ways of managing worker insurance costs. Using the right job title for each employee is very important. An employer will pay a fraction of the insurance for an office worker compared to a manufacturing plant worker. Some states have set up group plans where the rate will be much less to a business that can qualify.

    You may want to assign students to interview employers about the costs and problems associated with workers' compensation. Students could also research various insurance companies, trade associations, and businesses alike that sell workers' compensation insurance.

2.   On pages 301 and 302 of the textbook, an example is given showing the total payroll cost of an employee. In this example, payroll taxes add an additional 9.3% to gross wages. Students who are currently working may find it interesting to calculate what it really costs their employer for each hour they work.

Critical Thinking Activity

The groups formed in Chapter 8 to research the payroll methods may be re-formed. Have students report on the efficiencies and problems of the various payroll methods for end-of-quarter and end-of-year payroll processing.

Homework Suggestions

LO1 Study Guide Review Questions 1 through 6; Study Guide Exercise 1; End of Chapter Questions 1, 2, 3, 4.

LO2 Study Guide Review Question 7; Study Guide Exercises 2, 3; Study Guide Problem 6; End of Chapter Questions 5, 6, 7; Exercise 9-1A, 9-1B; Problem 9-7A, 9-7B.

LO3 Study Guide Review Questions 8, 9, 10; Study Guide Exercise 4; Study Guide Problem 7; End of Chapter Questions 8, 9, 10, 11; Problem 9-8A, 9-8B.

LO4 Study Guide Review Question 11; Study Guide Exercise 5; Study Guide Problem 8; End of Chapter Question 12.

Entire Chapter:
Mastery Problem and Challenge Problem.

Ten Questions Your Students Will Always Ask

1. Does the employer always contribute the same amount to FICA as the employee does?
2. In other words, self-employed people pay twice the tax even though they are only one person?
3. Taxable earnings for unemployment stop at $7,000.00; is the cutoff per person or per payroll?
4. Is the merit-rating system based on percentages over time, or does it take into account the employer's size or the state of the economy?
5. In other words, every time employees are paid, you have wages and salaries expense and payroll tax expense?
6. I have seen statements on employee bulletin boards in our state to the effect that employees don't contribute to unemployment insurance. However, isn't it true that an employer probably factors in unemployment insurance when determining pay scales?
7. Are there as many state forms as federal forms; what about city/county forms?
8. What are the penalties like if you don't file all these things on time?
9. Isn't workers' compensation insurance another factor in determining wage scales?
10. Who provides the insurance for extremely dangerous jobs; do they have to do so?

72

Learning Objectives

LO1 Explain the cash, modified cash, and accrual basis of accounting.

LO2 Describe special records for a professional service business using the modified cash basis.

LO3 Describe and use a combination journal to record transactions of a professional service business.

LO4 Post from the combination journal to the general ledger.

LO5 Prepare a work sheet, financial statements, and adjusting and closing entries for a professional service business.

Teaching Tip

➤ This chapter is optional. If you decide not to cover it, include the material on pages 332-337 with Chapter 7, Accounting For Cash. Review Questions 1 and 2, Exercises 10-1A and 10-1B can be used for reinforcement of this material.

LO1

❖ **Transparency Master 10-1 illustrates Figure 10-1 Cash Versus Accrual Accounting.**

❖ **Transparency Master 10-2 illustrates Figure 10-2 Comparison of Cash, Modified Cash, and Accrual Methods.**

❖ **PowerPoint Slides 10-1 through 10-72 present the Cash, Modified Cash, and Accrual Basis of Accounting**

I. Accrual Basis Versus Cash Basis **(See Figure 10-1 and Figure 10-2)**
    A.   **Accrual basis of accounting**
        1.   Revenues are recorded when earned.
            a)   Service is provided.
            b)   Product is sold.
        2.   Expenses are recorded when incurred.
            a)   Service is received.
            b)   Asset is consumed.
        3.   Measures income best for most businesses.

Teaching Tip

➤ Generally, comparisons between cash and accrual accounting are based on when to record revenues and expenses. It may also be helpful to compare the balance sheet accounts used under each method.

B.   **Cash basis of accounting**
1.   Revenues are recorded when cash is received.
2.   Expenses are recorded when cash is paid.
3.   Most individuals use it for tax purposes.

Teaching Tip

➤   Choosing an accounting method is an important decision for every business. Most small service businesses use the modified cash basis of accounting because it is workable for them. Such businesses do not want to record revenues for monies they have not received. Manufacturing and merchandising businesses generally use the accrual basis of accounting. Such companies need to match revenues and expenses very accurately. The cash basis of accounting is rarely used in business. Almost all companies have assets other than cash. To record these assets as expenses would not only be impractical but violate the tax laws for many businesses.

C.   **Modified cash basis of accounting**
1.   Uses cash basis for recording revenue and expenses.
2.   Assets acquired other than cash are recorded as assets instead of being recorded as expenses.

Teaching Tips

➤   Students often find the modified cash basis confusing. It may be helpful to point out that it is the same as the accrual basis except that receivables and payables are not recorded for revenues and operating expenses.

➤   By using the modified cash basis, a business can avoid distortions resulting from the purchase of plant assets.

In-Class Exercise: Complete Exercise 10-1A and 10-1B (30 minutes each)

LO2

II.   Accounting for a Professional Service Business
     A.   Often uses the modified cash basis of accounting.
     B.   Examples of professional service businesses:
          1.   Accounting
          2.   Law
          3.   Medicine
          4.   Engineering
     C.   No adjustments are made for accrued wages.
     D.   Accounts receivable is not recorded because services performed are not entered in accounting records until the cash is received.
          1.   Records must be kept to track clients and patients.
               a)   Appointment record **(See Figure 10-3)**
               b)   Ledger record **(See Figure 10-4)**

LO3

❖ **PowerPoint Slides 10-73 through 10-95 present the Combination Journal**

III. The **Combination Journal**
  A. **Special columns**
   1. Cash debits and credits.
   2. Frequently used accounts.
   3. Columns are totaled at the end of each month.

Teaching Tip

➢ Point out to your students that the special columns used in the combination journal are selected for each business based on which accounts are used most frequently.

  B. General Debit and General Credit columns
   1. Infrequently used accounts are entered here.
   2. Columns are totaled at the end of the month.

❖ **Transparency Master 10-3 illustrates Figure 10-7 Combination Journal: Modified Cash Basis.**

  C. Journalizing in a **combination journal (See Figure 10-5, Figure 10-6, and Figure 10-7)**
   1. General column transactions
     a) Enter the name of the debited account in the extreme left of the Description column.
     b) Enter the amount in the General Debit column.
     c) Enter the name of the account credited on the next line.
     d) Enter the amount in the General Debit column.
   2. General and special accounts transactions
     a) Enter the name of the general account in the Description column.
     b) Enter the amount in the **General Debit or Credit column.**
     c) Enter on the same line the amount of the debit or credit for the special account in the appropriate special account column.
   3. Special account transactions
     a) Enter the amounts in the appropriate special debit and credit columns.
     b) Do not enter anything in the Description column.
     c) Place a dash in the Posting Reference column to indicate the amount is not to be posted individually.

Teaching Tip

➢ Mention, again, that the special columns in the combination journal will be different for different businesses.

   4. Description column
     a) Enter the account titles for the General Debit and the General Credit columns.
     b) Identify specific creditors when assets are purchased on account.

75

c)   Identify the amounts forwarded when more than one page is used during an accounting period.

    D.   Proving the combination journal
        1.   Total and rule all columns at the end of the accounting period.
        2.   Sum of the debit columns should be equal to the sum of the credit columns.

LO4

❖   **Transparency Master 10-4 illustrates Figure 10-9 Posting to the Combination Journal.**

❖   **PowerPoint Slides 10-96 through 10-98 present Posting from the Combination Journal**

IV.   Posting from the Combination Journal **(See Figure 10-8 and Figure 10-9)**
    A.   General Columns
        1.   Enter "CJ" and the page number in each of the general ledger account's Posting Reference column.
        2.   Enter the account number in the **Posting Reference** column of the combination journal.
        3.   Post daily the accounts entered in the General Debit and Credit columns.

Teaching Tip

➢   Posting amounts in the General columns daily and the totals of the special columns less frequently means that the general ledger will be temporarily out of balance. This is okay. Everything will be posted before financial statements are prepared. This is a good place to review the posting process.

    B.   Special Columns
        1.   Total the special columns at the end of an accounting period.
        2.   Post the totals to the appropriate general ledger accounts.
        3.   Enter the account number beneath the column in parentheses.

❖   **Transparency Master 10-5 illustrates Figure 10-10 Determining the Cash Balance.**

    C.   Determining the cash balance   **(See Figure 10-10)**
        1.   Find the beginning cash balance.
        2.   Add the total cash debits.
        3.   Subtract the total cash credits.
        4.   Determine the result.

LO5

❖   **Transparency Master 10-6 illustrates Figure 10-11 Work Sheet for Ray Bonita, M.D.**

❖   **PowerPoint Slide 10-88 presents End of Period Work Sheet**

V.   Performing End-Of-Period Work for a Professional Service Business

    A.   Preparing a work sheet **(See Figure 10-11)**
    B.   Preparing financial statements **(See Figure 10-12)**
    C.   Preparing adjusting and closing entries **(See Figures 10-13 and 10-14)**

1. Use the General Debit column.
2. Use the General Credit column.

Teaching Tip

➤ Point out that the format for adjusting and closing entries in the combination journal is very similar to the one used in the general journal.

Learning Activity

A point should be made that businesses still using a manual accounting system, and the modified cash basis, rely on a combination journal or a derivation of it. Small businesses frequently use a combination journal or a One-Write system. A One-Write system enables a business to write a check and record the check at the same time. It can also be used for other tasks. It has many special columns that save time and paperwork. You may want to bring in and show the class a typical One-Write system.

Critical Thinking Activity

Randy Tupper opened a computer and multimedia repair business on June 1. Besides cash, he has the following special columns in his combination journal: Repair Fees, Supplies, and Wages Expense.
From the transactions that follow, indicate whether debits and credits should be journalized to and posted from a general column or a special column.

1. Invested $18,000 in the business
2. Purchased $4,500 of repair equipment on account
3. Paid office rent of $290
4. Received $350 for services rendered
5. Paid $320 for supplies
6. Paid wages of $120
7. Paid $800 on account
8. Withdrew $200 for personal use
9. Received $480 for services rendered
10. Paid utility bill of $400

Solution

Transaction	Debit	Credit
1.	Special	General
2.	General	General
3.	General	Special
4.	Special	Special
5.	Special	Special
6.	Special	Special
7.	General	Special
8.	General	Special
9.	Special	Special
10.	General	Special

LO1 Study Guide Review Questions 1 through 4; Study Guide Exercises 1, 2, 3; Study Guide Problem 5; End of Chapter Questions 1, 2.

LO2 End of Chapter Questions 3, 4.

LO3 Study Guide Review Questions 5 through 10; Study Guide Exercise 4; Study Guide Problem 6; End of Chapter Questions 5, 6, 7, 8, 9; Exercises 10-2A, 10-2B, 10-3A, 10-3B

LO4 Study Guide Review Questions 11, 12; End of Chapter Question 10.

LO5 Study Guide Problems 7, 8; End of Chapter Problems 10-4A, 10-4B, 10-5A, 10-5B

Entire Chapter:

Mastery Problem and Challenge Problem.

1. How big, in terms of income, should a business be to switch from modified cash to accrued?
2. Which method—accrued or modified cash—has the most paperwork?
3. Do we also learn how to keep the "special" records?
4. Does the combination journal get rid of the cash ledger account?
5. Who or what determines what special columns to use in the combination journal?
6. If a transaction is general and special, do you post both daily?
7. If you have ensured that each transaction balances, why do you total the general columns?
8. Do the totals in the general columns mean anything; i.e., are they posted?
9. Is the work sheet when you use a combination journal any different?
10. Is the closing process any different?

Chapter 11
Accounting for Sales and Cash Receipts

Learning Objectives

LO1   Describe merchandise sales transactions.
LO2   Describe and use merchandise sales accounts.
LO3   Describe and use the accounts receivable ledger.
LO4   Prepare a schedule of accounts receivable.

LO1

❖   **PowerPoint Slides 11-1 through 11-4 present Merchandising Businesses**

I.   Merchandise sales transactions
    A.   A **merchandising business** purchases merchandise such as clothing, furniture, or computers and sells that merchandise to customers.
    B.   A **sale** is a transfer of merchandise from one business or individual to another in exchange for cash or the promise to pay cash.
    C.   Retailer

Teaching Tip

➢   Emphasize the importance of cash register receipts, sales tickets, and sales invoices as <u>source documents</u> that provide the basis for recording sales transactions. Have students gather sales invoices, cash register receipts, credit memos, etc. from different types of businesses. Discuss the different features of each document.

    1.   Retail businesses generally sell to customers who enter a store.
    2.   Cash registers generate a receipt. **(See Figure 11-1)**
    3.   Most registers can print a summary of the day's sales activities.
    4.   Summaries can be used to journalize sales in the accounting records.
    5.   **Sales tickets** can be a written document created as evidence of a sale. **(See Figure 11-2)**

❖   **Transparency Master 11-1 illustrates Figure 11-3 Marketing Chain.**

    D.   Wholesaler **(See Figure 11-3)**
        1.   Wholesalers generally sell to retailers.

❖   **Transparency Master 11-2 illustrates Figure 11-4 Wholesale Sales Transaction Process.**

        2.   Documents generated by a wholesaler are **sales invoices** which often have three copies. **(See Figure 11-4 and Figure 11-5)**
            a)   One copy is sent to the customer as a bill of sale.
            b)   One copy is sent to accounting to record the sale.
            c)   One copy is shipped with the merchandise.

❖   PowerPoint Slide 11-5 presents the Credit Memo

  E. **Credit memo (See Figure 11-6)**
   1. **Sales returns** occur when merchandise is returned by customers for refunds.
   2. **Sales allowances** occur when seller grants price reductions because of defects or other problems with the merchandise.
   3. Seller issues credit memos for sales returns and sales allowances.

Teaching Tip

➢ Explain that a credit memorandum is given this name because the customer's account receivable is being <u>credited</u> to reduce the amount the customer owes.

In-Class Exercise: Complete Exercise 11-1A, 11-1B (5 minutes each)

LO2

❖   Transparency Master 11-3 illustrates Figure 11-7 Accounting for Merchandise Sales Transactions.

❖   PowerPoint Slides 11-6 through 11-36 present Merchandise Sales, Returns and Allowances and Discounts, with examples

II. Merchandise sales accounts **(See Figure 11-7)**
  A. Sales account
   1. Revenue account used to record sales of merchandise.
   2. Is credited for the selling price of the merchandise.
   3. Is used for both cash and credit sales.
  B. Sales tax payable account
   1. Liability account used to account for sales tax on merchandise sold to customers.
   2. Is credited for the taxes imposed on sales.
   3. Is debited when
    a) Sales taxes are paid to the proper taxing authority.
    b) Sales taxes are reduced for merchandise returned by customers.

Teaching Tip

➢ Remind students that Sales Tax Payable is a liability account. The sales tax simply is money collected by the business on behalf of the state. The account is similar to the various employee payroll tax liability accounts we used in Chapter 8 for amounts withheld from employee wages.

  C. Sales returns and allowances account
   1. Account is a contra-revenue account to which sales returns and sales allowances are debited.
   2. The amount debited excludes the sales tax.
   4. Sales Tax Payable is debited separately.
   5. Reported as a deduction from sales on Income Statement **(See Figure 11-8)**

Teaching Tip

➤ Explain that sales returns and allowances normally should be a very small percentage of sales. If Sales Returns and Allowances accumulates to a large balance, the business owner would want to investigate the cause.

      D.   Sales Discounts Account

❖ **Transparency Master 11-4 illustrates Figure 11-9 Credit Terms.**

          1.   **Cash discounts** are offered to customers to encourage prompt payment of sales on account. **(See Figure 11-9)**
          2.   Account is a contra-revenue account to which cash discounts allowed are debited.

Teaching Tip

➤ Point out that when merchandise is returned, the sales discount would be calculated on the sale amount <u>after</u> deducting the amount of the return. Also, if there is sales tax, the discount is calculated based on the amount of the sale excluding the sales tax.

          3.   Reported as a deduction from Sales on the income statement. **(See Figure 11-10)**

In-Class Exercise: Complete Exercise 11-3A, 11-3B (5 minutes each)

LO3

❖ **PowerPoint Slides 11-37 through 11-58 present Posting Sales Transactions**

III.   Journalizing and Posting Sales and Cash Receipts Transactions

❖ **Transparency Master 11-5 illustrates Figure 11-12 Posting Sales to the General Ledger.**

      A.   Posting to the general ledger **(See Figure 11-11 and Figure 11-12)**
          1.   **In the ledger account:**
              a)   Enter the date of the transaction in the Date Column.
              b)   Enter the amount of the debit or credit in the Debit or Credit column.
              c)   Enter the new balance in the Balance columns under Debit or Credit.
              d)   Enter the journal page number from which each transaction is posted in the Posting Reference column.
          2.   **In the journal:**
              a)   Enter the ledger account number in the Posting Reference column of the journal for each transaction that is posted.
              b)   Other sales transactions would be posted in the same manner.

In-Class Exercise: Complete Exercise 11-4A, 11-4B (15 minutes each)

B.   Subsidiary **accounts receivable ledger**
1.   Provides records of each customer's account.
2.   **Controlling account** is the summary accounts receivable account.
3.   Posted daily so the customer information is current.

Teaching Tips

➢   Emphasize that the accounts receivable subsidiary ledger is not part of the general ledger. It is a separate ledger.

➢   Note that, in a computerized system, the subsidiary accounts receivable ledger might be in account number order rather than alphabetical order.

❖   **Transparency 11-6 illustrates Figure 11-13 Posting Sales to the Accounts Receivable Ledger.**

C.   Posting to the accounts receivable ledger. **(See Figure 11-13)**
1.   **In the accounts receivable ledger account:**
      a)   Enter the date of the transaction in the Date column.
      b)   Enter the amount of the debit or credit in the Debit or Credit column.
      c)   Enter the new balance in the Balance column.
      d)   Enter the journal page number from which each transaction is posted in the Posting Reference column.
2.   **In the journal:**
      a)   Enter a slash (/) followed by a check mark (✓) in the Posting Reference column of the journal for each transaction that is posted.

Teaching Tips

➢   When discussing posting to the accounts receivable ledger, we recommend doing these three things:
- Emphasize the importance of posting the accounts receivable ledger daily so that information regarding individual customer accounts is readily available.
- Explain that the accounts receivable ledger can be posted either from the general journal or from the same source document used to enter the transactions in the general journal.
- Explain that in a computerized system a single entry of data into the system would update the journal, general ledger, and subsidiary ledger at the same time.

➢   Note that if the accounts receivable ledger is posted daily and the general ledger is posted at the end of the month, the accounts receivable ledger total will equal the general ledger Accounts Receivable total only at the end of the month. Use an example to demonstrate the temporary "imbalance" that could exist during the month.

❖   **Transparency Master 11-7 illustrates Figure 11-14 Accounting for Sales Returns and Allowances.**

D.   Sales returns and allowances **(See Figure 11-14)**
        1.   Require an entry in the general journal.
        2.   Posted daily
            a)   **In the accounts receivable ledger account:**
                (1)   Enter the date of the transaction in the Date column.
                (2)   Enter the amount of the debit or credit in the Debit or Credit column.
                (3)   Enter the new balance in the Balance column.
                (4)   Enter the journal page number from which each transaction is posted in the Posting Reference column.
            b)   **In the journal:**
                (1)   Enter a slash (/) followed by a check mark (✓) in the Posting Reference column of the journal for each transaction that is posted.

Teaching Tip

➢   Walk through the posting of a sales returns and allowances transaction to be sure students understand the dual posting of the credit to accounts receivable.

In-Class Exercise: Complete Problem 11-8A, 11-8B (5 minutes each)

❖   **Transparency Master 11-6 illustrates Figure 11-16 Posting Cash Receipts to the General Ledger and Accounts Receivable Ledger.**

IV.   Journalizing and Posting Cash Receipts
    A.   Cash receipts entered into General Journal **(See Figure 11-15)**
    B.   Posting to the General Ledger and Accounts Receivable Ledger **(See Figure 11-16)**
        1.   **In the accounts receivable ledger account:**
            a)   Enter the date of the transaction in the Date column.
            b)   Enter the amount of the debit or credit in the Debit or Credit column.
            c)   Enter the new balance in the Balance column.
            d)   Enter the journal page number from which each transaction is posted in the Posting Reference column.
        2.   **In the journal:**
            a)   Enter a slash (/) followed by a check mark (✓) in the Posting Reference column on the journal for each transaction that is posted.

❖   **Transparency Master 11-9 illustrates Figure 11-17 General Ledger and Accounts Receivable Ledger after Posting.**

    C.   After posting **(See Figure 11-17)**

In-Class Exercise: Complete Exercise 11-6A, 11-6B (15 minutes each)
In-Class Exercise: Complete Problem 11-10A, 11-10B (15 minutes each)

LO4

❖   **PowerPoint Slides 11-59 through 11-61 present Schedule of Accounts Receivable**

V.   **Schedule of Accounts Receivable (See Figure 11-18)**
    A.   Prepared to verify the sum of the accounts receivable ledger equals the controlling accounts receivable account balance.

Teaching Tip

➢   Have students compare the balances in the customer accounts in the accounts receivable subsidiary ledger with the amounts in the schedule of accounts receivable.

    B.   List of all customers with an account balance at the end of the month.
    C.   If the schedule does not agree with the accounts receivable balance, the error must be found.
        1.   Verify the total of the schedule.
        2.   Verify the postings to the accounts receivable ledger.
        3.   Verify the totals in the sales and cash receipts journal (if applicable).
        4.   Verify the posting to Accounts Receivable in the general ledger.

In-Class Exercise: Complete Exercise 11-7A, 11-7B (10 minutes each)
In-Class Exercise: Complete Problem 11-11A, 11-11B (10 minutes each)

Learning Activity

Have your students visit a wholesale business and a retail business and have them ask the accounting or bookkeeping department how they handle sales, both cash and credit, and then relate what they learned to this chapter.

Critical Thinking Activity

Ask students: When does a sale become a sale? Nine times out of ten, the students will say a sale is a sale when the merchant receives the cash. They say this because they are so attuned to the cash basis of accounting. A sale is recorded when the merchandise changes hands. There is a transfer of title and ownership.

Homework Suggestions

LO1   Study Guide Review Questions 1 through 8; Study Guide Exercises 1, 2; End of Chapter Questions 1, 2
LO2   Study Guide Review Questions 9 through 14; End of Chapter Question 3; Exercise 11-2A, 11-2B
LO3   Study Guide Review Questions 15, 16, 17, 18; Study Guide Exercises 3, 4, 5; Study Guide Problems 6, 8; End of Chapter Questions 4, 5, 6,7, 8; Exercise 11-5A, 11-5B; Problem 11-9A, 11-9B
LO4   Study Guide Review Questions 19, 20; Study Guide Problem 7; End of Chapter Question 9
Entire Chapter:
    Mastery Problem and Challenge Problem.

1. How much more complex is accounting for a merchandise business—since it is in the middle of a chain?
2. So now revenue has three parts—sales, returns, and discounts?
3. Why do you keep track of discounts if you never receive that money?
4. Same thing with allowances—you never received the money?
5. With these cash discounts, what if the seller offers 2/eom, n/60 and you buy on the 28th of the month—do you get only two or three days?
6. How often do we have to post sales on account?
7. Do all credit card companies charge the same fee to the retailer?
8. Do some businesses keep track of cash sales customers?
9. In a schedule of accounts receivable, do you list customers with a zero balance?
10. All this seems very labor-intensive; is there a more simplified way?

Chapter 12
Accounting for Purchases and Cash Payments

Learning Objectives

LO1 Define merchandise purchases transactions.
LO2 Describe and use merchandise purchases accounts and compute gross profit.
LO3 Describe and use the accounts payable ledger.
LO4 Prepare a schedule of accounts payable.

LO1

❖   **Transparency Master 12-1 illustrates Figure 12-1 Purchasing Process Documents**

❖   **PowerPoint Slides 12-1 through 12-12 present Merchandise Purchase Transactions**

I.   Merchandise Purchase Transactions **(See Figure 12-1)**
    A.   **Purchases**
        1.   Refers to merchandise acquired for sale in a retail business.
        2.   Procedures for purchasing and documentation vary, depending on the nature and size of the business.

Teaching Tips

➢   Purchasing procedures vary greatly across businesses. Have students describe the purchasing process where they work, and discuss differences identified.

➢   Walk through Figure 12-1 and explain the role each document plays in the purchasing process. Students often confuse the purposes of the purchase requisition and purchase order.

❖   **Transparency Master 12-2 illustrates Figure 12-2 Purchase Requisition.**

    B.   **Purchase requisition (See Figure 12-2)**
        1.   Form used to request the purchase of assets.
        2.   Authorized person prepares and sends form to the purchasing department.
        3.   Copies are sent to
            a)   Purchasing department
            b)   Accounting department
            c)   Kept by the department that prepared the requisition

Teaching Tip

➢   Explain that comparing the purchase invoice with the purchase requisition, purchase order, and receiving report is an example of good internal control. This procedure helps ensure that the business pays only for the goods it ordered and received, and at the correct price. Also emphasize the importance of the purchase invoice as a <u>source document</u> used to record purchase transactions.

❖ **Transparency Master 12-3 illustrates Figure 12-3 Purchase Order**

     C.   **Purchase order (See Figure 12-3)**
          1.   Written order to buy goods from a specific vendor.
          2.   Copies are sent to
              a)   Vendor to order the goods
              b)   Accounting department
              c)   Purchasing department
              d)   Originator of the purchase requisition
              e)   Receiving area

❖ **Transparency Master 12-4 illustrates Figure 12-4 Purchase Invoice**

     D.   Receiving report and the **purchase invoice (See Figure 12-4)**
          1.   **Receiving report** is prepared when goods are received.
          2.   **Invoice** is prepared by the seller and shipped to the buyer.
              a)   Accounting department compares the purchase invoice with the purchase requisition, purchase order, and receiving report.
              b)   Invoice is paid if everything is correct.

❖ **Transparency Master 12-5 illustrates Figure 12-5 Purchase Invoice with Trade Discount**

     E.   Cash and trade discounts **(See Figure 12-5)**
          1.   Cash discounts are available if the bill is paid within the discount period.
          2.   **Trade discounts** are percentage reductions from the total amount of the invoice.

Teaching Tip

➢   Explain the difference between cash and trade discounts. Cash discounts are given because a bill is paid promptly. Trade discounts are given because of the position of a business in the marketing chain. For example, a manufacturer will give a trade discount to a wholesaler because of the role the wholesaler plays in distributing the products to retailers. Emphasize that trade discount amounts are not entered into either the seller's or the buyer's accounts.

In-Class Exercise: Complete Exercise 12-1A, 12-1B (5 minutes each)
In-Class Exercise: Complete Exercise 12-2A, 12-2B (10 minutes each)

LO2

❖ **Transparency Master 12-6 illustrates Figure 12-6 Accounting for Merchandise Purchases Transactions**

❖ **PowerPoint Slides 12-13 through 12-58 present Merchandise Purchase Accounts and Computation of Gross Profit**

     II.   Merchandise Purchases Accounts **(See Figure 12-6)**

A. Purchases account
    1. Used to record the cost of merchandise purchased.
    2. Amount of each purchase is debited to the account.
B. Purchases returns and allowances
    1. Contra-purchases account used to record purchases returns and allowances.
    2. Reported as a deduction from Purchases on the income statement.
    3. Amount of each purchase returned or allowance granted is credited to the account.

Teaching Tip

➢ Caution students that Purchases Returns and Allowances is used to record only <u>merchandise</u> returns and allowances. If an asset other than merchandise is returned, that specific asset account is credited.

C. Purchases discounts account
    1. Used to record cash discounts on purchases.
    2. Reported as a deduction from Purchases on the income statement.
    3. Cash discounts on purchases are credited to the account.

Teaching Tips

➢ Point out that returns, allowances, and cash discounts are credited to separate accounts rather than directly to Purchases so that the business can keep track of these activities.

➢ Purchases discounts can be recorded using the <u>gross method</u> or the <u>net method</u>. The gross method is described in this chapter. The net method is described in the Appendix.

D. Freight-in account
    1. Used to report transportation charges on merchandise purchased.
    2. **FOB shipping point** means the transportation charges are paid by the buyer and are debited to the account.
    3. **FOB destination** means that transportation charges are paid by the seller and the freight-in account is not used.

Teaching Tips

➢ Students are accustomed to seeing advertising of products at a price "plus shipping and handling." Ask students what FOB terms are implied by such ads.

➢ Point out that the two shipping methods do not change the cost of the goods being purchased. FOB shipping point results in the purchase price of the goods and the shipping charges being separately identified on the books of the purchases. FOB destination does not result in separate identification. However, the seller of the goods includes the shipping charges in the cost of the items being purchased.

❖   **Transparency Master 12-7 illustrates Figure 12-7 Computation of Gross Profit**

E.   Computation of **gross profit** (also called **gross margin**) **(See Figure 12-7)**
1.   Net sales minus cost of goods sold equals gross profit.
2.   Merchandise available minus ending inventory equals **cost of goods sold** (also called **cost of merchandise sold**).
3.   Gross profit tells management the amount of sales revenue that are left to cover operation expenses.
4.   Computing gross profit
a)   Compute net sales
b)   Compute goods available for sale
c)   Compute cost of goods sold
d)   Compute gross profit

Teaching Tip

➢   Have students play the role of management. Assume that gross profit has shrunk because of competition. What expenses can be reduced to keep the business profitable? See if students are willing to eliminate jobs. This can provide a valuable real-world lesson.

In-Class Exercise: Complete Exercise 12-4A, 12-4B (10 minutes each)

LO3

❖   **Transparency Master 12-8 illustrates Figure 12-9 Posting Purchases to the General Ledger**

❖   **PowerPoint Slides 12-59 through 12-75 present Journalizing and Posting Purchases and Cash Payments Transactions**

III.   Journalizing and Posting Purchases and Cash Payments Transactions **(See Figure 12-8 and Figure 12-9)**
A.   Posting to the General Ledger
1.   **In the ledger account:**
a)   Enter the date of the transaction in the Date column
b)   Enter the amount of the debit or credit in the Debit or Credit column
c)   Enter the new balance in the Balance columns under Debit or Credit
d)   Enter the journal page number from which each transaction is posted in the Posting Reference column
2.   **In the journal:**
a)   Enter the ledger account number in the Posing Reference column of the journal for each transaction that is posted
b)   Other purchases transactions would be posted in the same manner
B.   Subsidiary **accounts payable ledger**
1.   Separate ledger containing an individual accounts payable for each supplier.
2.   Controlling accounts payable account is maintained in the general ledger.

❖   **Transparency Master 12-9 illustrates Figure 12-10 Posting Purchases to the Accounts Payable Ledger**

89

3.   Steps in posting process **(See Figure 12-10)**
    a)   **In the accounts payable ledger account:**
        (1)   Enter the date of the transaction in the Date column
        (2)   Enter the amount of the debit or credit in the Debit or Credit column
        (3)   Enter the new balance in the Balance column
        (4)   Enter the journal page number from which each transaction is posted in the Posting Reference column
    b)   **In the journal:**
        (1)   Enter a slash (/) followed by a check mark (✓) in the Posting Reference column of the journal for each transaction that is posted.

Teaching Tip

➢   Note that, if the accounts payable ledger is posted daily and the general ledger is posted at the end of the month, the accounts payable ledger total will equal the general ledger Accounts Payable total only at the end of the month. Use an example to demonstrate the temporary "imbalance" that could exist during the month.

In-Class Exercise: Complete Exercise 12-5A, 12-5B (15 minutes each)
In-Class Exercise: Complete Problem 12-9A, 12-9B (5 minutes each)
In-Class Exercise: Complete Problem 12-10A, 12-10B (10 minutes each)

❖   **Transparency Master 12-10 illustrates Figure 12-11 Accounting for Purchases Returns and Allowances**

    C.   Purchase returns and allowances **(See Figure 12-11)**
        1.   General journal entry is required.
        2.   Postings are made daily.
        a)   **In the accounts payable ledger account:**
            (1)   Enter the date of the transaction in the Date column.
            (2)   Enter the amount of the debit or credit in the Debit or Credit column
            (3)   Enter the new balance in the Balance column
            (4)   Enter the journal page number from which each transaction is posted in the Posting Reference column
        b)   **In the journal:**
            (1)   Enter a slash (/) followed by a check mark (✓) in the Posting Reference column of the journal for each transaction that is posted

Teaching Tip

➢   Walk through the posting of a purchases returns and allowances transaction to be sure students understand the dual posting of the debit to accounts payable.

IV.   Journalizing and Posting Cash Payments
       A.   Cash payments entered into general journal **(See Figure 12-12)**

❖   **Transparency Master 12-11 illustrates Figure 12-13 Posting Cash Payments to the General Ledger and Accounts Payable Ledger**

       B.   Posting to the general ledger and accounts payable ledger **(See Figure 12-13)**
             1.   **In the ledger account:**
                   a)   Enter the date of the transaction in the Date column
                   b)   Enter the amount of the debit or credit in the Debit or Credit column
                   c)   Enter the new balance in the Balance column
                   d)   Enter the journal page number from which each transaction is posted in the Posting Reference column
             2.   **In the journal:**
                   a)   Enter a slash (/) followed by a check mark (✓) in the Posting Reference Column of the journal for each transaction that is posted

❖   **Transparency Master 12-12 illustrates Figure 12-14 General Ledger and Accounts Payable Ledger after Posting**

       C.   After posting **(See Figure 12-14)**

In-Class Exercise: Complete Exercise 12-7A, 12-7B (15 minutes each)

LO4

❖   **PowerPoint Slides 12-76 and 12-77 present Schedule of Accounts Payable**

V.   **Schedule of Accounts Payable (See Figure 12-15)**
       A.   Prepared to verify that the sum of the accounts payable ledger balances equals the Accounts Payable balance.

Teaching Tip

➢   Have students compare the balances in the supplier accounts in the accounts payable subsidiary ledger with the amounts listed in the schedule of accounts payable.

       B.   Errors must be located and corrected.
             1.   Verify the total of the schedule.
             2.   Verity the posting to the accounts payable ledger.
             3.   Verify the totals in the purchases and cash payments journals (if applicable).
             4.   Verity the posting to Accounts Payable in the general ledger.

In-Class Exercise: Complete Exercise 12-8A, 12-8B (5 minutes each)
In-Class Exercise: Complete Problem 12-12A, 12-12B (10 minutes each)

Have your students visit one or more of their favorite retail stores and have them ask the bookkeeping department how and when the store's purchases are made and how and when their payments are made and then relate their findings to this chapter.

It may seem to students that a lot of paperwork is generated to purchase goods. Have students discuss the reasons for preparing purchase requisitions, purchase orders, receiving reports, and purchase invoices. Part of the discussion should center on the problems that could result by not preparing each type of paperwork. If necessary, point out that the reports prepared and received by the buyer act as checks and balances in the purchasing procedure. These chains of authorization are used to prevent the unauthorized purchase of goods and other property. These reports also act as source documents for the data entered in the company's accounting systems.

LO1 Study Guide Review Questions 1 through 7; Study Guide Exercises 1, 2, 3, 4, 5; End of Chapter Questions 1, 2.

LO2 Study Guide Review Questions 8 through 12; Study Guide Exercise 6; End of Chapter Questions 3, 4; Exercise 12-3A, 12-3B.

LO3 Study Guide Review Questions 13 through 17; Study Guide Exercise 7; Study Guide Problems 8, 11; End of Chapter Questions 5, 6, 7, 8, 9; Exercise 12-6A, 12-6B; Problems 12-11A, 12-11B.

LO4 Study Guide Review Question 18; Study Guide Problems 9, 10; End of Chapter Question 10.

Entire Chapter:
Mastery Problem and Challenge Problem.

1. Are purchases sort of treated like expenses?
2. Once again, is there a really good reason for all this paperwork?
3. So, the invoice comes from our supplier to us, the retailer?
4. If we pay in time, why do we keep track of the discounts?
5. Do we have an account for trade discounts?
6. How often do we have to post purchases on account?
7. Is freight-in an expense account or something else?
8. Why, if we don't pay for it, do we account for an allowance on a purchase?
9. In the schedule of accounts payable, do you list all of your suppliers or just the ones you owe?
10. Really, it seems as if all this journalizing and posting is getting out of hand. Can't it be simplified?

Learning Objectives

LO1 Describe the net-price method of recording purchases.
LO2 Record purchases and cash payments using the net-price method.

LO1

❖ **PowerPoint Slides 12Apx-1 and 12Apx-2 present Recording Purchases Methods**

I.   Net-Price Method
    A.   Alternative approach to Gross-Price method of accounting for purchases.
    B.   Purchases are recorded at the net amount, assuming that all available cash discounts will be taken.

LO2

❖ **PowerPoint Slides 12Apx-3 through 12Apx-12 present Comparison of Gross-Price and Net-Price Methods**

II.   Compare **Gross-Price Method** and **Net-Price Method**
    A.   Purchase merchandise for $100 on account with credit terms of 2/10, n/30
        1.   Gross-Price Method
            a)   Debit Purchases $100
            b)   Credit Accounts Payable $100
        2.   Net-Price Method
            a)   Debit Purchases $98 ($100 - $2) ($100 × 2% = $2 discount)
            b)   Credit Accounts Payable $98

III.   Payment made within discount period
    A.   Gross-Price Method
        1.   Debit Accounts Payable $100
        2.   Credit Cash $98
        3.   Credit Purchases Discount $2
    B.   Net-Price Method
        1.   Debit Accounts Payable $98
        2.   Credit Cash $98

IV.   Payment made after discount period expires
    A.   Gross-Price Method
        1.   Debit Accounts Payable $100
        2.   Credit Cash $100
    B.   Net-Price Method
        1.   Debit Accounts Payable $98

        2.   Debit Purchases Discounts Lost $2
            a)   temporary owner's equity account
            b)   normal debit balance
        3.   Credit Cash $100

In-Class Exercise: Complete Exercise 12Apx-1A (15 minutes)

Homework Suggestions

LO2   Study Guide Apx. Exercise; End of Appendix Exercise 12Apx-1B

Learning Objectives

LO1 Describe, explain the purposes of, and identify transactions recorded in special journals.

LO2 Describe and use the sales journal.

LO3 Describe and use the cash receipts journal.

LO4 Describe and use the purchases journal.

LO5 Describe and use the cash payments journal.

LO1

❖ **PowerPoint Slides 13-1 through 13-6 present Special Journals**

I.   Special Journals **(See Figure 13-1)**

Teaching Tip

➤   Point out that special journals also make it possible to divide up the work of recording different types of transactions.

    A.   Sales Journal
    B.   Cash Receipts Journal
    C.   Purchases Journal
    D.   Cash Payments Journal

In-Class Exercise: Complete Exercise 13-1A, 13-1B (15 minutes each)

LO2

❖ **PowerPoint Slides 13-7 through 13-30 present the Sales Journal**

II   **Sales Journal (See Figure 13-2, Figure 13-3, and Figure 13-4)**
    A.   Special journal used to record only sales on account.
        1.   Record sales on account by entering the following information.
            a)   Date
            b)   Sale number
            c)   Customer
            d)   Dollar amounts
        2.   Retailers - columns used
            a)   Accounts Receivable is debited.
            b)   Sales is credited.
            c)   Sales Tax Payable is credited.
        3.   Wholesalers - a single amount column headed Accounts Receivable. Debit/Sales Credit is used since sales tax does not apply to goods purchased for resale.

Teaching Tip

➤ Actually enter the five transactions on pages 457, 458 in a general journal and in a sales journal in class and compare the time required.

In-Class Exercise: Complete Exercise 13-2A, 13-2B (10 minutes each)

❖ **Transparency Master 13-1 illustrates Figure 13-5 Posting the Sales Journal to the General Ledger**

    B.   Posting from the Sales Journal **(See Figure 13-5)**
        1.   **In the sales journal, monthly:**
            a)   Total the amount columns, verify that the total of the debit column equals the total of the credit columns, and rule the columns.
        2.   **In the ledger account, monthly:**
            a)   Enter the date of the transaction in the Date column
            b)   Enter the amount of the debit or credit in the Debit or Credit column
            c)   Enter the new balance in the Balance columns under Debit or Credit.
            d)   Enter an S and the journal page number in the Posting Reference column.
        3.   **In the sales journal, monthly:**
            a)   Enter the ledger account number immediately below the column totals for each account that is posted.

❖ **Transparency Master 13-2 illustrates Figure 13-6 Posting the Sales Journal to the Accounts Receivable Ledger**

    C.   Posting to the Accounts Receivable Ledger **(See Figure 13-6)**
        1.   **In the accounts receivable ledger account, daily:**
            a)   Enter the date of the transaction in the Date column
            b)   Enter the amount of the debit or credit in the Debit or Credit column.
            c)   Enter the new balance in the Balance column.
            d)   Enter an S and the journal page number in the Posting Reference column.
        2.   **In the sales journal, daily:**
            a)   Enter a check mark (✓) in the Posting Reference column of the journal for each transaction that is posted.

In-Class Exercise: Complete Problem 13-6A, 13-6B (15 minutes each)

LO3

❖ **Transparency Master 13-3 illustrates Figure 13-7 Northern Micro Cash Receipts Journal (left and right sides)**

❖ **PowerPoint Slides 13-31 through 13-74 present the Cash Receipts Journal**

    III.   **Cash Receipts Journal (See Figure 13-7 and Figure 13-8)**
        A.   Special journal used to record only cash receipts.
            1.   Record cash receipts by entering the following information:
                a)   Date

b)   Account credited (identify customer for any payment received)

c)   Dollar amounts

2.   Transactions include collections from customers, cash sales, bank credit card sales, receipt of revenue, and loans from bank.

Teaching Tips

➢   The last transaction illustrated involves signing a note to borrow money from the bank. If students ask what a note is, tell them this is simply a formal promise to repay the loan. The topic is covered fully in Chapter 18.

➢   As with the sales transactions, actually enter several cash receipt transactions in a general journal and cash receipts journal in class and compare the time required.

➢   Emphasize that cash sales are recorded in the cash receipts journal, not the sales journal. Students often think that all sales are recorded in the sales journal.

❖   **Transparency Master 13-4 illustrates Figure 13-9 Posting the Cash Receipts Journal to the General Ledger**

B.   Posting from the cash receipts journal **(See Figure 13-9)**

1.   **In the ledger account, daily:**

a)   Enter the date of the transaction in the Date column

b)   Enter the amount of the debit or credit in the Debit or Credit column.

c)   Enter the new balance in the Balance columns under Debit or Credit.

d)   Enter a CR and the journal page number in the Posting Reference Column.

2.   **In the cash receipts journal, daily:**

a)   Enter the ledger account number in the Posting Reference column for each account that is posted.

3.   **In the cash receipts journal, monthly:**

a)   Total the amount columns, verify that the total of the debit columns equals the total of the credit columns, and rule the columns.

4.   **In the ledger account, monthly:**

a)   Enter the date in the Date column.

b)   Enter the amount of the debit or credit in the Debit or Credit column.

c)   Enter the new balance in the Balance columns under Debit or Credit.

d)   Enter a CR and the journal page number in the Posting Reference column.

5.   **In the cash receipts journal, monthly:**

a)   Enter the ledger account number immediately below the column totals for each account that is posted.

b)   Enter a check mark (✓) in the Posting Reference column for the cash sales and bank credit card sales, and immediately below the General Credit column.

In-Class Exercise: Complete Exercise 13-3A, 13-3B (15 minutes each)

❖ **Transparency Master 13-5 illustrates Figure 13-10 Posting the Cash Receipts Journal to the Accounts Receivable Ledger**

    C.   Posting to the Accounts Receivable ledger (**See Figure 13-10**)

        1.   **In the accounts receivable ledger account, daily:**

            a)   Enter the date of the transaction in the Date column

            b)   Enter the amount of the debit or credit in the Debit or Credit column.

            c)   Enter the new balance in the Balance column.

            d)   Enter a CR and the journal page number in the Posting Reference column.

        2.   **In the cash receipts journal, daily:**

            a)   Enter a check mark (✓) in the Posting Reference column of the journal for each transaction that is posted.

Teaching Tip

➢   Have students explain every posting reference in the cash receipts journal, including when the posting was made and to what account. This will help you determine whether they understand the posting process.

LO4

❖ **PowerPoint Slides 13-75 through 13-86 present the Purchases Journal**

IV.   **Purchases Journal (See Figure 13-11 and Figure 13-12)**

    A.   Special journal used to record only purchases of merchandise on account.

        1.   Each recording consists of

            a)   Date

            b)   Invoice number

            c)   Supplier (from whom purchased)

            d)   Dollar amount

Teaching Tips

➢   Emphasize that the purchases journal illustrated here is used to record only merchandise purchased on account. Purchases of supplies, equipment, etc. must be recorded elsewhere. You might want to point out that there is another type of purchases journal, often called an acquisitions journal, which can be used to record all types of purchases on account.

➢   Actually enter the five transactions on text page 467 in a general journal and in a purchases journal in class and compare the time required.

In-Class Exercise: Complete Exercise 13-4A, 13-4B (10 minutes each)

❖ **Transparency Master 13-6 illustrates Figure 13-13 Posting the Purchases Journal to the General Ledger**

    B.   Posting the Purchases Journal (**See Figure 13-13**)

        1.   **In the purchases journal, monthly:**

            a)   Total and rule the amount column.

2.　**In the ledger account, monthly:**
　　a)　Enter the date in the Date column.
　　b)　Enter the amount of the debit or credit in the Debit or Credit column.
　　c)　Enter the new balance in the Balance columns under Debit or Credit.
　　d)　Enter a P and the journal page number in the Posting Reference column.
3.　**In the purchases journal, monthly:**
　　a)　Enter the Purchase and Accounts Payable account numbers immediately below the column total.

Teaching Tip

➢　Have students compare the purchases journal posting process in Figure 13-13 with the sales journal posting process in Figure 13-5. Seeing the similarity of the two systems can help students understand both of them.

❖　**Transparency Master 13-7 illustrates Figure 13-14 Posting the Purchases Journal to the Accounts Payable Ledger**

C.　Posting to the Accounts Payable Ledger (**See Figure 13-14**)
　1.　**In the accounts payable ledger account, daily:**
　　a)　Enter the date of the transaction in the Date column.
　　b)　Enter the amount of the debit or credit in the Debit or Credit Column.
　　c)　Enter the new balance in the Balance column.
　　d)　Enter a P and the journal page number in the Posting Reference column.
　2.　**In the purchases journal, daily:**
　　a)　Enter a check mark (✓) in the Posting Reference column of the journal for each transaction that is posted.

In-Class Exercise: Complete Problem 13-10A, 13-10B (15 minutes each)

LO5

❖　**Transparency Master 13-8 illustrates Figure 13-15 Northern Micro Cash Payments Journal (left and right sides)**

❖　**PowerPoint Slides 13-87 through 13-110 present the Cash Payments Journal**

V.　**Cash Payments Journal (See Figure 13-15)**
　A.　Types of cash payments
　　1.　Payment of expense
　　2.　Cash purchase
　　3.　Payment of accounts payable
　　4.　Payment of notes payable
　　5.　Withdrawal by an owner
　B.　Cash payments are recorded with
　　1.　Date
　　2.　Check number
　　3.　Account debited
　　4.　Dollar amounts

99

<u>Teaching Tip</u>

➢ Emphasize that cash purchases are recorded in the cash payments journal, not in the purchases journal.

In-Class Exercise: Complete Exercise 13-5A, 13-5B (15 minutes each)

❖ **Transparency Master 13-9 illustrates Figure 13-16 Posting the Cash Payments Journal to the General Ledger.**

C.   Posting the cash payments journal **(See Figure 13-16)**
   1.   **In the ledger account, daily:**
        a)   Enter the date of the transaction in the Date column.
        b)   Enter the amount of the debit or credit in the Debit or Credit column.
        c)   Enter the new balance in the Balance columns under Debit or Credit.
        d)   Enter a CP and the journal page number in the Posting Reference column.
   2.   **In the cash payments journal, daily:**
        a)   Enter the ledger account number in the Posting Reference column for each account that is posted.
   3.   **In the cash payments journal, monthly:**
        a)   Total the amount columns, verify that the total of the debit columns equals the total of the credit columns, and rule the columns.
   4.   **In the ledger account, monthly:**
        a)   Enter the date in the Date column.
        b)   Enter the amount of the debit or credit in the Debit or Credit column.
        c)   Enter the new balance in the Balance columns under Debit or Credit.
        d)   Enter a CP and the journal page number in the Posting Reference column.
   5.   **In the cash payments journal, monthly:**
        a)   Enter the ledger account number immediately below the column totals for each account that is posted.
        b)   Enter a check mark (✓) in the Posting Reference column for the cash purchases, and immediately below the General Debit column.

❖ **Transparency Master 13-10 illustrates Figure 13-17 Posting the Cash Payments Journal to the Accounts Payable Ledger**

D.   Posting to the Accounts Payable ledger **(See Figure 13-17)**
   1.   **In the accounts payable ledger account, daily:**
        a)   Enter the date of the transaction in the Date column.
        b)   Enter the amount of the debit or credit in the Debit or Credit column.
        c)   Enter the new balance in the Balance column.
        d)   Enter a CP and the journal page number in the Posting Reference column.
   2.   **In the cash payments journal, daily:**
        a)   Enter a check mark (✓) in the Posting Reference column of the journal for each transaction that is posted.

Teaching Tip

➤ Have students explain every posting reference in the cash payments journal, including when the posting was made and to what account. This will help you determine whether they understand the posting process.

Learning Activity

1. With their books closed, have the students write in detail 2 transactions that would be recorded in a sales journal, 3 transactions that would be recorded in a cash receipts journal, and 1 transaction that would be recorded in a general journal.

2. With their books closed, have the students write in detail 2 transactions that would be recorded in a purchases journal, 3 transactions that would be recorded in a cash payments journal, and 1 transaction that would be recorded in a general journal.

Critical Thinking Activity

Ask your students if they think that a special journal should be created for sales returns and allowances for a large retailer. Would their response be different or the same if the retailer sold on account, like a building supply store?

Homework Suggestions

LO1 Study Guide Review Questions 1, 2; Study Guide Exercise 1; End of Chapter Question 1.

LO2 Study Guide Review Questions 3, 4, 5, 6; Study Guide Exercise 2; End of Chapter Questions 2, 3, 4.

LO3 Study Guide Review Questions 7, 8, 9; Study Guide Exercise 3; Study Guide Problems 7, 8; End of Chapter Questions 5, 6, 7; Problems 13-7A, 13-7B, 13-8A, 13-8B.

LO4 Study Guide Review Questions 10 through 14; Study Guide Exercise 4; Study Guide Problem 9; End of Chapter Questions 8, 9, 10; Problem 13-9A, 13-9B.

LO5 Study Guide Review Questions 15, 16, 17, 18; Study Guide Exercise 5; Study Guide Problem 10; End of Chapter Questions 11, 12, 13; Problem 13-11A, 13-11B.

Entire Chapter:
Problem 13-12A and 13-12B; Mastery Problem and Challenge Problem.

1. Are these the journals that are supposed to save time and be more efficient?
2. Do all retail or merchandise businesses use all of these journals?
3. Only credit sales go in the sales journal, so a large retail store may not have one?
4. What about sales returns and allowances? Do they go in the sales journal?
5. Are <u>all</u> cash receipts entered into the cash receipts journal?
6. If a sales journal is used and a cash receipts journal is used, then the sales account would get two credit postings a period?
7. Are purchases of office supplies or cleaning supplies entered into the purchases journal?
8. Are <u>all</u> cash payments entered into the cash payments journal?
9. If cash and credit purchases of merchandise are made, then the purchases account would get postings from both the cash payments and purchases journal?
10. Should we always verify the totals in each journal before we post if we verified with each transaction?

Chapter 14
The Voucher System

Learning Objectives

LO1 Describe how a voucher system is used to control expenditures.
LO2 Prepare a voucher.
LO3 Describe and use a voucher register.
LO4 Describe the payment process using a voucher system.
LO5 Describe and use a check register and prepare a schedule of vouchers payable.
LO6 Account for returns, allowances, and partial payments.

LO1

❖ **PowerPoint Slides 14-1 through 14-6 present Internal Control of Expenditures**

I.   Internal Control of Expenditures
    A.   Elements of **Internal Control**

Teaching Tip

➤   Emphasize to students that internal controls are important in <u>every business</u>, regardless of its size. The main effect of size on internal controls is that in larger businesses, the internal controls need to be more formal and tend to be more costly.

        1.   Segregation of duties
            a)   Different employees should be responsible for different parts of a transaction.
            b)   Employees who account for transactions should not also have custody of the assets.

Teaching Tip

➤   Explain to students the fundamental internal control concept that no employee should be in a position to take business assets for personal use and conceal the fact that they did so.

        2.   Authorization procedures and related responsibilities
            a)   Every business activity should be properly authorized.
            b)   Signed documents should show who is responsible for every business transaction.

Teaching Tip

> Note how just requiring employees to sign off on various documents improves performance because the employees know they will be held directly responsible for their actions.

  3. Adequate documents and records
    a) Accounting documents and records should be used to support all business transactions.
    b) Documentation should be prenumbered, used in sequence, and subsequently accounted for.

Teaching Tips

> Stress the importance of the trail of documents in the internal control system. These documents are the evidence underlying the entries in the journals and ledgers.

> Students who have experience with a small business might see the voucher system as cumbersome and expensive. Admit to these students that a formal voucher system is most appropriate for medium and large size businesses. The volume of transactions in a business must be sufficient to warrant the cost of such a system.

❖ **Transparency Master 14-1 illustrates Figure 14-1 Voucher System—Purchasing Process**
❖ **PowerPoint Slides 14-7 through 14-16 present the same information**
❖ **PowerPoint Slide 14-17 presents the Voucher System**

  B. **Voucher System (See Figure 14-1)**
    1. Control technique that requires that every acquisition and subsequent payment be supported by an approved voucher.
    2. **Vouchers** are documents which show that an acquisition is proper and the payment is authorized.
    3. Using vouchers in the purchasing system.
      a) Vouchers are prepared if the purchases requisition, purchase order, receiving report, and purchase invoice agree.
      b) Vouchers are entered in a special journal called the voucher register.
      c) Each purchase should be supported by five documents:
        (1) Voucher
        (2) Purchase invoice
        (3) Receiving report
        (4) Purchase order
        (5) Purchase requisition

Teaching Tips

> Flowcharts are generally viewed as a more effective way than a narrative to describe and document an accounting system. The flowcharts used here follow standard conventions in use of symbols, but are highly simplified. For example, the document symbol is used for all documents, the rectangle is

used for all actions and processes, and the inverted triangle depicts a document file. To keep the flowcharts very simple, however, the flow of a copy of the purchase requisition and purchase order to the vouchers payable section is not clearly shown. You might want to explain the standard flowcharting symbols and the simplification to the students.

➢ Take a moment to explain the difference between a supplier invoice and a monthly statement. Students are familiar with paying monthly statements, so they have trouble understanding paying individual invoices. Point out that a business can make several payments to the same supplier in a single month for different purchases.

In-Class Exercise: Complete Exercise 14-1A, 14-1B (5 minutes each)

LO2

❖ **PowerPoint Slides 14-18 through 14-30 present Preparing a Voucher**

II. Preparing a Voucher
   A. Procedures followed when a purchase invoice is received **(See Figure 14-2)**
      1. Compare the invoice with purchase requisition, purchase order, and receiving report to determine that
         a) The quantity was requested, ordered, and received.
         b) The price and credit terms are correct.
      2. Judge whether the purchases are appropriate for the business.
      3. Verify all computations on the invoice.

In-Class Exercise: Complete Exercise 14-2A, 14-2B (10 minutes each)

❖ **Transparency Master 14-2 illustrates Figure 14-3 Voucher**

   B. Procedures in preparing the voucher **(See Figure 14-3)**
      1. On the front side of the voucher, insert
         a) Voucher date
         b) Invoice terms
         c) Due date
         d) Supplier name and address
         e) Invoice date
         f) Description of items purchased
         g) Invoice amount less any discounts
      2. On the back, insert the accounts and the amounts to be debited.
      3. The voucher clerk signs the voucher and has it approved by the voucher supervisor.
      4. When the voucher is paid, the "Payment" section on the back is completed.

LO3

❖   **PowerPoint Slides 14-31 through 14-51 present the Voucher Register**

III.   **Voucher Register (See Figure 14-4)**

      A.   A voucher register is a special journal used to record purchases of all types of assets and services.

Teaching Tip

➢   Remind students that the voucher register is simply another type of special journal. As such, the columns used depend on the number and types of transactions that are common for a particular business.

      B.   Vouchers are recorded in the voucher register with its date, voucher number, person or business to whom the voucher is issued, and the dollar amounts of debits and credits.

      C.   Filing unpaid vouchers

           1.   Vouchers are attached to their supporting documents after they are entered in the register.

           2.   Voucher packets are filed in the **unpaid vouchers file** by due date.

Teaching Tip

➢   Emphasize the benefit of filing vouchers by due date. This enables management to plan for its cash needs and to take advantage of cash discounts for timely payment of bills. The person responsible for cash payments must closely monitor the unpaid vouchers file.

❖   **Transparency Master 14-3 illustrates Figure 14-5 Posting Voucher Register to General Ledger**

      D.   Posting from the voucher register **(See Figure 14-5)**

Teaching Tip

➢   Walk through the posting process in Figure 14-5. Have students explain exactly <u>what</u> is being posted, <u>where</u>, and <u>when</u>.

           1.   On a daily basis:

                a)   Post each amount from the General Debit column to the appropriate general ledger account.

                b)   Insert the date in the Date column and the initials "VR" and the voucher register page number in Posting Reference column of each general ledger account.

                c)   Insert the general ledger account numbers in the Posting Reference column of the General Debit column of the voucher register.

           2.   At the end of each month:

                a)   Total the amount columns, verify that the total of the debit columns equals the total of the credit column, and rule the columns.

                b)   Post each column total except the General Debit column to the general ledger account indicated in the column headings.

	c)	Insert the date in the Date column and the initials "VR" and the voucher register page number in the Posting Reference column of each ledger account.
	d)	Insert the general ledger account numbers immediately below each column total except the General Debit column.
	e)	Insert a check mark immediately below the General Debit column.

In-Class Exercise: Complete Exercise 14-3A, 14-3B (15 minutes each)

LO4

❖ **Transparency Master 14-4 illustrates Figure 14-6 Voucher System—Payment Process**

❖ **PowerPoint Slides 14-52 through 14-59 present the Payment Process**

IV. The Payment Process Using A Voucher System **(See Figure 14-6)**
   A. Paying the voucher
      1. Vouchers are pulled from the unpaid voucher file on the due date and given to the people responsible for preparing and signing checks.
      2. Cashiers review each voucher and supporting documents to see if the expenditure is proper.
      3. The check is prepared, signed, and sent to the supplier.

Teaching Tip

➢ Stress the absolutely critical function of the check signer in reviewing the voucher and supporting documents. If checks are written only with clear evidence that goods or services were ordered, received, and billed for the proper amount, management has good control of its expenditures.

   B. **Voucher checks (See Figure 14-7)**
      1. Checks with space for entering data about the voucher being paid.
      2. Statement attached indicates the invoice being paid and any deductions.
   C. **Paid vouchers file**
      1. Where vouchers are filed numerically or by supplier.
      2. Vouchers and supporting documents are canceled to indicate payment.

In-Class Exercise: Complete Exercise 14-4A, 14-4B (5 minutes each)

LO5

❖ **PowerPoint Slides 14-60 through 14-68 present the Check Register**

V. **Check Register (See Figure 14-8)**
   A. Special journals used to record all checks in a voucher system.
   B. Columns
      1. Vouchers Payable Debit
      2. Purchases Discount Credit
      3. Cash Credit
   C. Check is recorded by entering its date, check number, payee, voucher number, and dollar amount.

D.   Date of payment and check number are entered into the payment portion of the voucher register for the appropriate voucher number **(See Figure 14-9)**

❖   **Transparency Master 14-5 illustrates Figure 14-10 Posting Check Register to General Ledger**

E.   Posting from the check register **(See Figure 14-10)**
1.   Total the amount columns, verify that the total of debit columns equals the total of the credit columns, and rule the columns.
2.   Post each column total to the general ledger account indicated in the columns headings.
3.   Insert the date in the Date column and the initials "CK" and the check register page number in the Posting Reference column of each ledger account.
4.   Insert the general ledger account numbers immediately below each column total.

Teaching Tip

➢   Students often forget to enter the payment of a voucher in the <u>voucher register</u>, in addition to the check register. Carefully walk through this dual recording process in class and explain how these two journals are linked.

In-Class Exercise: Complete Exercise 14-5A, 14-5B (15 minutes each)

F.   Schedule of vouchers payable **(See Figure 14-11)**
1.   Used to verify that the sum of the individual amounts owed to the creditors equals the vouchers payable account balance.
2.   Schedule is prepared from either the voucher register or the unpaid vouchers file.
3.   If the schedule total and voucher payable account balance do not agree, the error must be found and corrected.
      a)   Verify the total of the schedule.
      b)   Review the voucher register or the unpaid vouchers file to be sure none were missed or counted twice.
      c)   Verify the totals in the voucher and check registers.
      d)   Verify the postings to Vouchers Payable in the general ledger.

In-Class Exercise: Complete Exercise 14-6A, 14-6B (10 minutes each)

LO6

❖   **PowerPoint Slides 14-69 through 14-81 present Accounting for Returns, Allowances, and Partial Payments**

VI.   Accounting for returns, allowances, and partial payments
    A.   Purchase returns and allowances
       1.   Complete return
          a)   Note the return on the voucher, attach the credit memo, and place the voucher in the paid vouchers file.
          b)   Note the return in the Payment column of the voucher register.
          c)   Make a journal entry to record the return.

2. Partial return
    a)   Note the return on the voucher, attach the credit memo, and return the voucher to the unpaid vouchers file.
    b)   Note the return in the voucher register in the Payment column.
    c)   Make a general journal entry to record the return.
    d)   When the voucher is paid for the original amount less the return, note the payment in the Payment column of the voucher register.

Teaching Tips

➢   Call attention to the subtle difference in the "R" notation for the full vs. partial return. The "R" notation is sufficient for the full return because the Vouchers Payable Cr. shows the amount returned. For the partial return, the amount returned needs to be included in the notation.

➢   When making the entry for a return or allowance, the general journal entry really reverses the original entry in the voucher register. Stress that the credit is to Purchases, not Purchases Returns and Allowances.

B.   Partial payments
    1.   Planned
        a)   Separate vouchers are prepared for each payment.
        b)   Each voucher and payment is then recorded in the voucher register and check register.
    2.   After the voucher is created and entered
        a)   Original voucher is canceled and new vouchers are created.
        b)   Make a general journal entry to cancel the original voucher.
        c)   Make a notation in the Payment column of the voucher register.
        d)   New vouchers are prepared and entered in the voucher register.

In-Class Exercise: Complete Exercise 14-7A, 14-7B (20 minutes each)

Learning Activity

The area of internal controls over cash provides an excellent opportunity for a field trip. The students are to go to a retail store or a restaurant and observe the controls that the establishment uses over cash. They are also encouraged to talk to the manager about other controls that may not be obvious. The cash register will probably appear on everyone's write-up. Hopefully, students will spot some lack of controls as well as controls over tips, making change, deposits, etc.[**]

[**] Dorcas E. Berg, "Field Trips," *Great Ideas in Teaching Introductory Accounting,* South-Western College Publishing, Cincinnati, Ohio, 1996, p. 202.

Critical Thinking Activities

---

1.   Ask students who have job experience to discuss the internal controls they have found in place in their various jobs. The discussion can be very meaningful if students can list examples of strong and weak internal controls.

2. Ask students to think of situations in which a business' assets could be in jeopardy because of a lack of internal control. Student teams could research incidents in which weak internal controls have resulted in ethical or legal problems for a business or its owners. Use the discussion to emphasize how the voucher system can be a tool that can be used to make sure all the checks and balances are in place.

Homework Suggestions

LO1   Study Guide Review Questions 1 through 8; Study Guide Exercises 1, 4; End of Chapter Questions 1, 2.

LO2   Study Guide Review Questions 9, 10; Study Guide Exercises 2, 3; End of Chapter Question 3.

LO3   Study Guide Review Questions 11 through 16; Study Guide Problem 6; End of Chapter Questions 4, 5, 6; Problem 14-8A, 14-8B.

LO4   Study Guide Review Questions 17, 18; Study Guide Exercise 5; End of Chapter Question 7.

LO5   Study Guide Review Questions 19, 20, 21; Study Guide Problems 7, 9; End of Chapter Questions 8, 9, 10; Problems 14-9A, 14-9B, 14-10A, 14-10B.

LO6   Study Guide Review Questions 22, 23, 24; Study Guide Problem 8; End of Chapter Questions 11, 12

Entire Chapter:
Problem 14-11A, 14-11; Mastery Problem and Challenge Problem.

Ten Questions Your Students Will Always Ask

1.   Would medium or large company be determined by income/profit or by number of employees?
2.   Isn't a voucher system extremely expensive?
3.   A voucher is a separate piece of paper authorizing payment?
4.   In other words, all purchases are recorded in the voucher register?
5.   Are all cash payments—including drawing—recorded in the voucher register?
6.   Do we still maintain subsidiary ledgers for our suppliers?
7.   How is a messed up (coffee spills, mistakes) voucher or voucher check voided?
8.   It would seem that the "R" for return with a number for the amount would be difficult to include in that small box—wouldn't that lead to mistakes?
9.   So, a return goes to the general journal, the voucher register, and the voucher payable ledger?
10.   In other words, a voucher can pay a voucher?

Learning Objectives

LO1 Prepare an adjustment for merchandise inventory using the periodic inventory system

LO2 Prepare an adjustment for unearned revenue

LO3 Prepare a work sheet for a merchandising business

LO4 Journalize adjusting entries for a merchandising business

LO5 Prepare adjusting journal entries under the perpetual inventory system

LO1

❖   **Transparency Master 15-1 illustrates Figure 15-1 Review of Entries for Purchase and Sale of Merchandise**

❖   **PowerPoint Slides 15-1through 15-31 present Adjustment for Merchandise Inventory**

I.   Adjustment for Merchandise Inventory using the periodic inventory system **(See Figure 15-1)**

   A.   **Physical Inventory**

      1.   Quantity of inventory on hand at the end of an accounting period is determined by taking a physical count of the goods on hand.

Teaching Tip

➢   Students may wonder why no entries are made to the merchandise inventory account as goods are bought and sold. If the class is ready, you might briefly describe the perpetual inventory method that will be addressed in Chapter 19. With the use of computers, more businesses are moving to the perpetual method.

❖   **Transparency Master 15-2 illustrates Figure 15-2 Two-Step Adjustment for Merchandise Inventory**

      2.   Adjustments **(See Figure 15-2)**

         a)   Beginning inventory is removed by crediting Merchandise Inventory. Income Summary is debited because this amount is used in the calculation of cost of goods sold. "Cost of Goods Sold" is an expense on the income statement.

         b)   Ending inventory is entered by debiting Merchandise Inventory. Income Summary is credited because this amount also is used in the calculation of cost of goods sold. After making the second adjustment, the balance in Merchandise Inventory reflects the inventory on hand at the end of the accounting period.

❖   **Transparency Master 15-3 illustrates Figure 15-3 Calculation of Cost of Goods Sold Using Information in the Income Statement Columns of the Work Sheet**

      c)   Both the debit and credit made to the income summary account are extended to the Adjusted Trial Balance and Income Statement columns. This provides the information to compute Cost of Goods Sold. **(See Figure 15-3)**

Teaching Tips

➢ You might use the transparency of Figure 15-6 to emphasize the proper extensions of the new accounts related to merchandise, income summary, and unearned revenue.

➢ Review carefully the cost of goods sold calculation. Remind students that the cost of goods sold calculation appears on the income statement. Also explain that the ending inventory value appears on the balance sheet.

In-Class Exercise: Complete Exercise 15-1A, 15-1B (5 minutes each)
In-Class Exercise: Complete Exercise 15-2A, 15-2B (10 minutes each)
In-Class Exercise: Complete Exercise 15-5A, 15-5B (5 minutes each)

LO2

❖ **PowerPoint Slides 15-32 through 15-47 present Adjustment for Unearned Revenue and Expanded Chart of Accounts**

II.   Adjustment for **Unearned Revenue (See Figure 15-4)**
      A.   Cash is received in advance from a customer
            1.   A business receiving money in advance owes the customer a product or a service, or must refund the money.
            2.   Unearned revenue is reported on the balance sheet as a liability.

Teaching Tip

➢ Businesses that receive cash in advance must be careful in accounting for this unearned revenue. If a store receives a deposit for goods to be ordered, it must not confuse the deposit with a sale. Remember, a sale occurs when goods are transferred from one party to another. The deposit in this example is unearned revenue.

In-Class Exercise: Complete Exercise 15-3A, 15-3B (10 minutes each)

      B.   Expanded chart of accounts **(See Figure 15-5)**
            1.   **Contra-revenue accounts**
                a)   Sales returns and allowances
                b)   Sales discounts
            2.   **Contra-cost accounts**
                a)   Purchase returns and allowances
                b)   Purchase discounts
             3.   Interest expense is classified as "Other Expense" instead of being listed under operating expenses.

LO3

❖ Transparency Master 15-4 illustrates Figure 15-6 Overview of Worksheet for a Merchandising Business

❖ PowerPoint Slides 15-48 through 15-69 present Preparing a Work Sheet

III. Preparing a Work Sheet for a Merchandising Business (See Figure 15-6)

❖ Transparency Master 15-6 illustrates Figure 15-9 Step 1: Completion of the Trial Balance Columns

    A.   Prepare the trial balance. (See Figure 15-9)

❖ Transparency Master 15-5 illustrates Figure 15-8 Adjusting Entries for Northern Micro

❖ Transparency Master 15-7 illustrates Figure 15-10 Step 2: Preparation of the Adjustments

    B.   Prepare the adjustments. (See Figure 15-7, Figure 15-8, and Figure 15-10)

Teaching Tips

➢ Use this opportunity to reinforce the importance of adjusting entries. Only two new adjustments are introduced in this chapter (a, b, and h). The other adjustments were explained in Chapter 5. Ask students why these entries are necessary.

➢ When demonstrating the inventory/income summary adjustments, it may be helpful to draw an "X" in the adjustment columns to demonstrate that the credit of "old" inventory becomes a debit in income summary and the debit of "new" inventory becomes a credit in income summary.

❖ Transparency Master 15-8 illustrates Figure 15-11 Step 3: Extensions to the Adjusted Trial Balance Columns

    C.   Prepare the adjusted trial balance. (See Figure 15-11)

❖ Transparency Master 15-9 illustrates Figure 15-12 Step 4: Extensions to the Income Statement and Balance Sheet Columns; and Step 5: Completing the Work Sheet and Computing Net Income

    D.   Extend the adjusted trial balance to the Income Statement and Balance Sheet columns. (See Figure 15-12)

    E.   Total the Income Statement and Balance Sheet columns to compute the net income or net loss. (See Figure 15-12)

LO4

IV. Adjusting Entries (See Figure 15-13)

    A.   Making the adjusting entries on the work sheet has no effect on the actual accounts in the journal.

    B.   Adjusting entries must be journalized and then posted to the ledger accounts.

LO5

V.   Perpetual Inventory System **(See Figure 15-14)**
    A.   Inventory Purchased
        1.   Merchandise Inventory account is debited
        2.   Cash or accounts payable is credited
    B.   Inventory Sold
        1.   Cash or accounts receivable is debited
        2.   Sales is credited
        3.   Cost of goods sold is debited
        4.   Merchandise Inventory is credited
    C.   Adjusting entries
        1.   When actual inventory (by physical count) is less than the inventory account balance
            a)   Cost of goods sold is debited
            b)   Merchandise Inventory is credited
        2.   When actual inventory (by physical count) is more than the inventory account balance
            a)   Merchandise Inventory is debited
            b)   Cost of goods sold is credited

In-Class Exercise: Complete Exercise 15-7A, 15-7B (5 minutes each)

Learning Activity

Have the students name the businesses in the community that would have unearned revenue.

Critical Thinking Activity

Ask students who have had experience taking inventory to relate their experiences. Ask them to consider how the procedures used helped ensure the accuracy of the inventory count. What procedures were weak in ensuring the accuracy of the inventory count?

Homework Suggestions

LO1   Study Guide Review Questions 1 through 8, 12; Study Guide Exercises 1, 2; End of Chapter Questions 1, 3.

LO2   Study Guide Review Questions 9, 10, 11, 13; Study Guide Exercise 3; End of Chapter Questions 4, 5.

LO3   Study Guide Review Questions 14, 15, 16, 17; Study Guide Problem 7; End of Chapter Questions 6, 7; Exercise 15-4A, 15-4B.

LO4   Study Guide Exercise 4; Study Guide Problem 8; End of Chapter Exercise 15-6A, 15-6B.

LO5   Study Guide Review Questions 18, 19; Study Guide Exercises 5, 6; End of Chapter Question 8; End of Chapter Exercise 15-8A, 15-8B.

Entire Chapter:
    Problems 15-9A, 15-9B, 15-10A, 15-10B, 15-11A, 15-11B, 15-12A, 15-12B; Mastery Problem and Challenge Problem.

1. In other words, in the inventory column, the beginning inventory is zeroed out with a credit and the new inventory is entered as a debit?
2. In "cost of goods sold," whose costs are we talking about?
3. In other words, cost of goods sold is an expense?
4. Does all of the cost of goods sold information go on the income statement—or just the total?
5. Is this the same income summary account we used in closing in a service business?
6. On the work sheet, only income summary is extended?
7. Other than income summary playing a part, is the work sheet the same as in a service business?
8. Is unearned revenue an opposite of revenue earned on account?
9. Why do we journalize the inventory/income summary—they just balance each other out?
10. In the Appendix, why is the expense method used if the end of period report shows the supplies and other prepaid items that remain as assets?

Learning Objectives

LO1 Use the expense method of accounting for prepaid expenses
LO2 Make the appropriate adjusting entries when the expense method is used for prepaid expenses

LO1

❖ **PowerPoint Slides 15Apx-1 through 15Apx-6 present the Expense Method of Accounting for Prepaid Items**

I.   The Expense Method
    A.   Supplies and other prepaid items are entered as expenses when purchased.
        1.   Purchased office supplies for $425
            a)   Debit Office Supplies Expense $425
            b)   Credit Cash $425
        2.   Purchased 3-year insurance policy for $6000
            a)   Debit Insurance Expense $6000
            b)   Credit Cash $6000
    B.   Adjust the expense accounts at end of each accounting period to record the unused portions as assets.

LO2

❖ **PowerPoint Slides 15Apx-7 through 15Apx-11 present Adjusting Entries Under the Expense Method**

II.   Adjusting Entries Under the Expense Method
    A.   Supplies - inventory indicates $150 remaining on hand at end of accounting period
        1.   Debit Office Supplies $150
        2.   Credit Office Supplies Expense $150
    B.   Insurance - at end of first year, one third has expired and two thirds remain ($6000/3 × 2=$4000)
        1.   Debit Prepaid Insurance $4000
        2.   Credit Insurance Expense $4000

III.   After Adjusting Entries Have Been Posted
    A.   Supplies
        1.   Office Supplies Expense has a $275 debit balance.
        2.   Office Supplies has a $150 debit balance.
    B.   Insurance
        1.   Insurance Expense has a $2000 debit balance.
        2.   Prepaid Insurance has a $4000 debit balance.

Teaching Tip

➤   It would be a good idea to work several examples of the expense method on the board as this "change" in treating supplies and other prepaid items may cause some difficulty, even with your best students.

IV.   Asset and Expense Methods
      A.   Asset method
          1.   Prepaid item is first debited to an asset account.
          2.   Amount consumed during the accounting period is debited to an expense account at the end of the accounting period.
      B.   Expense method
          1.   Original amount is debited to expense account.
          2.   The portion not consumed is debited to an asset account at end of accounting period.

In-Class Exercise: Complete Exercise 15Apx-1A (5 minutes)
In-Class Exercise: Complete Exercise 15Apx-1B (5 minutes)

Homework Suggestions

LO2   Study Guide Exercises 1, 2

Learning Objectives

LO1 Prepare a single-step and multiple-step income statement for a merchandising business

LO2 Prepare a statement of owner's equity

LO3 Prepare a classified balance sheet

LO4 Compute standard financial ratios

LO5 Prepare closing entries for a merchandising business

LO6 Prepare reversing entries

LO1

I.   Preparation of Financial Statements **(See Figure 16-1)**

Teaching Tip

➢   It might be helpful to review the income statement for a service business before introducing one for a merchandising business.

    A.   Income Statement

❖   **Transparency Master 16-1 illustrates Figure 16-2 Single-Step Income Statement**

❖   **PowerPoint Slides 16-1 through 16-17 present the Income Statement**

        1.   **Single-step income statement (See Figure 16-2)**
            a)   List all revenues and their totals first.
            b)   List all expense items and their totals second.
            c)   List net income last.

❖   **Transparency Master 16-2 illustrates Figure 16-3 Multiple-Step Income Statement**

        2.   **Multiple-step income statement (See Figure 16-3)**
            a)   Gross sales are listed.
            b)   Sales returns, allowances, and discounts are subtracted to produce **net sales.**

In-Class Exercise: Complete Exercise 16-1A, 16-1B (10 minutes each)

            c)   Purchases minus purchases returns and allowances equals **net purchases**
            d)   Beginning inventory plus net purchases plus freight in minus ending inventory equals **cost of goods sold**
            e)   Net Sales minus cost of goods sold equals **gross profit** (also called **gross margin**).

      f)   Gross profit minus operating expenses equals **income from operations** (also called **operating income**).

          (1)   **Selling expenses** include such expenses as
- (a)   Sales salary expense
- (b)   Sales commissions expense
- (c)   Delivery expense
- (d)   Advertising expense
- (e)   Bank credit card expense
- (f)   Depreciation expense—store equipment and fixtures

          (2)   **General expenses** include such expenses as
- (a)   Office salaries expense
- (b)   Office supplies expense
- (c)   Rent expense
- (d)   Telephone expense
- (e)   Insurance expense
- (f)   Utilities expense

      g)   Other revenues are added and other expenses are subtracted to arrive at net income or net loss.

Teaching Tip

➢   By showing other revenue and other expenses separately, it is possible to show income from operations. This makes it easier for the reader to see how the business is doing in its main business activity.

LO2

❖   **Transparency Master 16-3 illustrates Figure 16-4 Capital Account for Gary L. Fishel**

❖   **Transparency Master 16-4 illustrates Figure 16-5 Statement of Owner's Equity**
❖   **PowerPoint Slides 16-18 through 16-23 present the same information**

      B.   Statement of owner's equity (**See Figure 16-4 and Figure 16-5**)

Teaching Tip

➢   The statement of owner's equity is the same for service and merchandising businesses.

      1.   Summarizes all changes in owner's equity during the period.
- a)   Additional investments
- b)   Net income
- c)   Net loss
- d)   Withdrawals

      2.   The balances shown on this statement also appear in the owner's equity section of the balance sheet.

LO3

❖ Transparency Master 16-5 illustrates Figure 16-6 Balance Sheet for Northern Micro

❖ PowerPoint Slides 16-24 through 16-38 present the Balance Sheet

 C. The balance sheet **(See Figure 16-6)**
  1. **Current assets**
   a) Includes cash and all other assets expected to be converted into cash within one year or the normal operating cycle of the business, whichever is longer.
   b) An **operating cycle** is the length of time required to buy inventory, sell it, and collect the cash.
   c) Types of current assets listed by liquidity:
    (1) Cash
    (2) Receivable
    (3) Merchandise inventory
    (4) Prepaid expenses
   d) **Liquidity** refers to the speed with which an asset can be converted into cash.
  2. **Property, plant, and equipment**
   a) Assets expected to be used for more than one year in the operations of a business.
   b) Types of property, plant, and equipment
    (1) Land
    (2) Buildings
    (3) Office equipment
    (4) Store equipment
    (5) Delivery equipment
   c) Accumulated depreciation amounts are deducted from the original cost of depreciable assets to provide **book value** (also called **undepreciated cost**).
  3. **Current liabilities**
   a) Obligations due within one year or the normal operating cycle of the business, whichever is longer.
   b) Types of current liabilities
    (1) Notes Payable
    (2) Accounts Payable
    (3) Wages Payable
    (4) Taxes Payable
    (5) Unearned Subscriptions Payable
    (6) Mortgage Payable--current portion

Teaching Tip

➢ Point out that the current portion of long-term debt, the amount due within one year, is reported as a current liability. The remainder is reported under long-term liabilities.

  4. **Long-term liabilities**
   a) Obligations that extend beyond a single operating cycle.

b) **Mortgage Payable** is an account used to reflect an obligation that is secured by a **mortgage** on certain property.

5. Owner's equity reflects the net worth of a business

In-Class Exercise: Complete Problem 16-9A, 16-9B (15 minutes each)

LO4

❖ **PowerPoint Slides 16-39 through 16-65 present Financial Statement Analysis**

II. Financial Statement Analysis
    A. Balance sheet analysis
        1. **Working capital**, current assets minus current liabilities, represents the amount available for current obligations.
        2. **Current ratio**, ratio of current assets to current liabilities, is a measure of the firm's ability to pay its current liabilities.
        3. **Quick ratio**, ratio of **quick assets** (cash, accounts receivable, and temporary investments) to current liabilities, is a second measure of a firm's ability to pay its current liabilities.
    B. **Interstatement analysis**
        1. **Return on owner's equity**, the ratio of net income to average owner's equity.
        2. **Accounts receivable turnover**
            a) Ratio of net credit sales for the period to average accounts receivable.
            b) Computes the number of times accounts receivables turned over or were collected during the accounting period.
            c) The number of days in a year (365) divided by the number of times accounts receivable were collected in a year indicates the **average collection period.**
        3. **Inventory turnover**
            a) Ratio of cost of goods sold for the period to average inventory.
            b) Computes the number of times the merchandise turns over, or is sold, during the accounting period.
            c) The number of days in a year (365) divided by the number of times inventory turned over equals **average days to sell inventory**.

Teaching Tips

➤ Stress the importance of comparing ratios with past performance and with other firms in the same industry. Information on industry averages is available in various publications from Dun & Bradstreet, Standard & Poor's, and Moody's.

➤ It may be helpful to point out that these ratios, and how they are determined, are one of the reasons management majors should take accounting.

In-Class Exercise: Complete Exercise 16-7A, 16-7B (30 minutes each)

LO5

❖ **Transparency Master 16-6 illustrates Figure 16-7 Closing Entries for a Merchandising Business**

❖ **Transparency Master 16-7 illustrates Figure 16-8 The Closing Process**

❖ **PowerPoint Slides 16-66 through 16-76 present Closing Entries**

III. Closing Entries **(See Figure 16-7 and Figure 16-8)**
 A. Steps used to prepare closing entries for a merchandising firm:
  1. All income statement accounts with credit balances are debited, with an offsetting credit to Income Summary.

Teaching Tip

➢ Point out that the first closing entry closes the revenue and contra-cost (purchases returns and allowances and purchases discounts) accounts.

  2. All income statement accounts with debit balances are credited, with an offsetting debit to Income Summary.

Teaching Tip

➢ Point out that the second closing entry closes the expense and contra-revenue (sales returns and allowances) accounts.

  3. The resulting balance in Income Summary, which is the net income or loss for the period, is transferred to the owner's capital account.
  4. The balance in the owner's drawing account is transferred to the owner's capital account.

❖ **Transparency Master 16-8 illustrates Figure 16-9 Post-Closing Trial Balance**

 B. **Post-closing trial balance (See Figure 16-9)**
  1. Prepared after the temporary owner's equity accounts have been closed.
  2. Purpose is to prove the general ledger is in balance

Teaching Tip

➢ Stress that the post-closing trial balance must be prepared by taking the balances from the general ledger accounts. Some students may want to use the balances reported on the work sheet. This defeats the purpose of making sure that all adjusting and closing entries were entered and posted correctly.

LO6

❖   Transparency Master 16-9 illustrates Figure 16-10 Adjusting, Closing, and Reversing Entries for Wages

❖   Transparency Master 16-10 illustrates Figure 16-11 Which Adjusting Entries to Reverse?

❖   Transparency Master 16-11 illustrates Figure 16-12 Reversing Entry for Northern Micro

❖   PowerPoint Slides 16-77 through 16-85 present Reversing Entries

IV.   **Reversing Entries (See Figure 16-10, Figure 16-11 and Figure 16-12)**
   A.   Reversing entries are the opposite of adjusting entries.
   B.   Reverse only adjusting entries that increase an asset or liability account from a zero balance.

Teaching Tip

➢   Once again, it may be helpful to work several reversing entries on the board since, with some students, it is a difficult idea to grasp.

In-Class Exercise: Complete Exercise 16-5A, 16-5B (10 minutes each)

Learning Activities

1.   Have students compare financial statements for a service business and a merchandising business. Write a report about the similarities and differences between the statements.

2.   Ask groups of students to select a particular type of business. Then have them go to the library to determine what industry the business is in and prepare a list of industry averages for the ratios discussed in this chapter. In class, you might discuss why the ratios differ across industries.

3.   Bring in annual reports from businesses and have students see the financial statements as they appear in these reports.

Critical Thinking Activity

Stress to the students that financial statement analysis is an integral part of being an accountant. Financial ratios can be used as tools by the accountant in helping explain what the numbers mean to the business owner. Provide several examples of ratios with enough detail that students can analyze the results. Discuss what the ratio means to (1) the short-run success of the business, (2) the long-term consequences if the ratio remains unchanged, and (3) the manager responsible for the results. A good example is accounts receivable turnover. This ratio illustrates the number of times receivables are collected in an accounting period, usually a year. For example, if a company has a turnover ratio of 9, you can divide it into 365 days. That means the company is collecting its money approximately every forty days. If the terms of invoicing are 2/10, n/30, then someone in collections is lagging. The owner can find out why and hopefully improve the cash flow of the business.

123

LO1 Study Guide Review Questions 1 through 6; Study Guide Exercise 1; Study Guide Problem 5; End of Chapter Question 1; Exercise 16-3A, 16-3B.

LO2 Study Guide Review Question 7.

LO3 Study Guide Review Questions 8 through 12; Study Guide Exercise 2; Study Guide Problem 7.

LO4 Study Guide Review Questions 13 through 18; Study Guide Exercise 3; Study Guide Problem 8; End of Chapter Questions 2, 3; Problem 16-10A, 16-10B.

LO5 Study Guide Review Questions 19, 20; End of Chapter Questions 4, 5, 6; Exercise 16-4A, 16-4B.

LO6 Study Guide Review Questions 21,22; Study Guide Exercise 4; Study Guide Problem 6; End of Chapter Questions 7, 8, 9; Exercise 16-6A, 16-6B; Problem 16-8A, 16-8B.

Entire Chapter:

Mastery Problem and Challenge Problem.

Ten Questions Your Students Will Always Ask

1.   The multiple-step income statement and the classified balance sheet certainly have a lot of steps and columns—how important is form?
2.   What kind of other revenues or expenses could a merchandise company have?
3.   If the telephone is used by the sales staff to make sales, is the telephone bill expense split into two parts?
4.   What about inventory that has been around over a year—current or not?
5.   What about inventory of out-of-style items or obsolete items—how are they treated?
6.   Where does mortgage interest show up on these statements?
7.   An additional investment in owner's equity must be determined from the ledger account and not last period's ending equity—is this correct?
8.   Are there other types of long-term liabilities that businesses may have?
9.   In other words, we have to look to the income summary ledger account to determine the amount to close to capital?
10.   Are there any accounts other than wages payable that can be reversed?

Alternative Chapters 11 and 12

These alternative Chapters 11 and 12 are provided as a special feature in the 18th edition. They cover the same topics as Chapters 11-13 in the main text. The key difference is that Sales and Cash Receipts and the related special journals are presented in a single chapter (Chapter 11). Similarly, Purchases and Cash Payments and the related special journals also are presented as a single chapter (Chapter 12). Some users have expressed a preference for coverage of these topics in this form, and these two alternative chapters do so. If these two chapters are used, there is no need to cover Chapters 11-13 in the main text.

Learning Objectives

LO1 Describe merchandise sales transactions.
LO2 Describe and use merchandise sales accounts.
LO3 Describe and use the sales journal and accounts receivable ledger.
LO4 Describe and use the cash receipts journal and accounts receivable ledger.
LO5 Prepare a schedule of accounts receivable.

LO1

❖ **PowerPoint Slides 11-1 through 11-4 present Merchandising Businesses**

I. Merchandise sales transactions
    A. A **merchandising business** purchases merchandise such as clothing, furniture, or computers and sells that merchandise to customers.
    B. A **sale** is a transfer of merchandise from one business or individual to another in exchange for cash or the promise to pay cash.
    C. Retailer

Teaching Tip

➢ Emphasize the importance of cash register receipts, sales tickets, and sales invoices as <u>source documents</u> that provide the basis for recording sales transactions. Have students gather sales invoices, cash register receipts, credit memos, etc. from different types of businesses. Discuss the different features of each document.

    1. Retail businesses generally sell to customers who enter a store.
    2. Cash registers generate a receipt. **(See Figure 11-1)**
    3. Most registers can print a summary of the day's sales activities.
    4. Summaries can be used to journalize sales in the accounting records.

❖ **Transparency Master 11-1 illustrates Figure 11-2 Sales Ticket.**

    5. **Sales tickets** can be a written document created as evidence of a sale. **(See Figure 11-2)**

❖ **Transparency Master 11-2 illustrates Figure 11-3 Marketing Chain.**

    D. Wholesaler **(See Figure 11-3)**
        1. Wholesalers generally sell to retailers.

❖ **Transparency Master 11-3 illustrates Figure 11-4 Wholesale Sales Transaction Process.**

❖ **Transparency Master 11-4 illustrates Figure 11-5 Sales Invoice.**

2.   Documents generated by a wholesaler are **sales invoices** which often have three copies. **(See Figure 11-4 and Figure 11-5)**
         a)   One copy is sent to the customer as a bill of sale.
         b)   One copy is sent to accounting to record the sale.
         c)   One copy is shipped with the merchandise.

❖   **Transparency Master 11-5 illustrates Figure 11-6 Credit memo.**

❖   **PowerPoint Slide 11-5 presents the Credit Memo.**

     E.   **Credit memo (See Figure 11-6)**
         1.   **Sales returns** occur when merchandise is returned by customers for refunds.
         2.   **Sales allowances** occur when seller grants price reductions because of defects or other problems with the merchandise.
         3.   Seller issues credit memos for sales returns and sales allowances.

Teaching Tip

➢   Explain that a credit memorandum is given this name because the customer's account receivable is being <u>credited</u> to reduce the amount the customer owes.

In-Class Exercise: Complete Exercise ALT11-1A, ALT11-1B (5 minutes each)

LO2

❖   **Transparency Master 11-6 illustrates Figure 11-7 Accounting for Merchandise Sales Transactions.**

❖   **PowerPoint Slides 11-6 through 11-36 present Merchandise Sales, Returns and Allowances and Discounts, with examples**

II.   Merchandise sales accounts **(See Figure 11-7)**
     A.   Sales account
         1.   Revenue account used to record sales of merchandise.
         2.   Is credited for the selling price of the merchandise.
         3.   Is used for both cash and credit sales.
     B.   Sales tax payable account
         1.   Liability account used to account for sales tax on merchandise sold to customers.
         2.   Is credited for the taxes imposed on sales.
         3.   Is debited when
             a)   Sales taxes are paid to the proper taxing authority.
             b)   Sales taxes are reduced for merchandise returned by customers.

Teaching Tip

➢   Remind students that Sales Tax Payable is a liability account. The sales tax simply is money collected by the business on behalf of the state. The account is similar to the various employee payroll tax liability accounts we used in Chapter 8 for amounts withheld from employee wages.

C. Sales returns and allowances account
   1. Account is a contra-revenue account to which sales returns and sales allowances are debited.
   2. The amount debited excludes the sales tax.
   3. Sales Tax Payable is debited separately.
   4. Reported as a deduction from sales on Income Statement **(See Figure 11-8)**

Teaching Tip

➢   Explain that sales returns and allowances normally should be a very small percentage of sales. If Sales Returns and Allowances accumulates to a large balance, the business owner would want to investigate the cause.

D. Sales Discounts Account
   1. **Cash discounts** are offered to customers to encourage prompt payment of sales on account. **(See Figure 11-9)**
   2. Account is a contra-revenue account to which cash discounts allowed are debited.

Teaching Tip

➢   Point out that when merchandise is returned, the sales discount would be calculated on the sale amount <u>after</u> deducting the amount of the return. Also, if there is sales tax, the discount is calculated based on the amount of the sale excluding the sales tax.

   3. Reported as a deduction from Sales on the income statement. **(See Figure 11-10)**

In-Class Exercise: Complete Exercise ALT11-3A, ALT11-3B (5 minutes each)

LO3

❖ **Transparency Master 11-7 illustrates Figure 11-11 Sales Entered in General Journal.**

❖ **Transparency Master 11-8 illustrates Figure 11-12 Northern Micro Sales Journal.**

❖ **PowerPoint Slides 11-37 through 11-61 present the Sales Journal**

III   **Sales Journal (See Figure 11-11, Figure 11-12, and Figure 11-13)**
   A. Special journal used to record only sales on account.
      1. Record sales on account by entering the following information.
         a) Date
         b) Sale number
         c) Customer
         d) Dollar amounts
      2. Retailers - columns used
         a) Accounts Receivable is debited.
         b) Sales is credited.
         c) Sales Tax Payable is credited.

3. Wholesalers - a single amount column headed Accounts Receivable. Debit/Sales Credit is used since sales tax does not apply to goods purchased for resale.

Teaching Tip

➢   Actually enter the five transactions on pages 9, 10 in a general journal and in a sales journal in class and compare the time required.

In-Class Exercise: Complete Exercise ALT11-4A, ALT11-4B (15 minutes each)

❖ **Transparency Master 11-9 illustrates Figure 11-14 Posting the Sales Journal to the General Ledger**

B. Posting from the Sales Journal **(See Figure 11-14)**
   1. **In the sales journal, monthly:**
      a) Total the amount columns, verify that the total of the debit column equals the total of the credit columns, and rule the columns.
   2. **In the ledger account, monthly:**
      a) Enter the date of the transaction in the Date column
      b) Enter the amount of the debit or credit in the Debit or Credit column
      c) Enter the new balance in the Balance columns under Debit or Credit.
      d) Enter an S and the journal page number in the Posting Reference column.
   3. **In the sales journal, monthly:**
      a) Enter the ledger account number immediately below the column totals for each account that is posted.

❖ **Transparency Master 11-12 illustrates Figure 11-15 Posting the Sales Journal to the Accounts Receivable Ledger**

C. Posting to the subsidiary Accounts Receivable Ledger **(See Figure 1-15)**
   1. Provides records of each customer's account.
   2. **Controlling account** is the summary accounts receivable account.
   3. Posted daily so the customer information is current.
   4. **In the accounts receivable ledger account, daily:**
      a) Enter the date of the transaction in the Date column
      b) Enter the amount of the debit or credit in the Debit or Credit column.
      c) Enter the new balance in the Balance column.
      d) Enter an S and the journal page number in the Posting Reference column.
   5. **In the sales journal, daily:**
      a) Enter a check mark (✓) in the Posting Reference column of the journal for each transaction that is posted.

Teaching Tips

➢   Emphasize that the accounts receivable subsidiary ledger is not part of the general ledger. It is a separate ledger.

➢ Note that, in a computerized system, the subsidiary accounts receivable ledger might be in account number order rather than alphabetical order.

➢ When discussing posting to the accounts receivable ledger, we recommend doing these three things:
- Emphasize the importance of posting the accounts receivable ledger daily so that information regarding individual customer accounts is readily available.
- Explain that the accounts receivable ledger can be posted either from the sales or general journal or from the same source document used to enter the transactions in the general journal.
- Explain that in a computerized system a single entry of data into the system would update the journal, general ledger, and subsidiary ledger at the same time.

➢ Note that if the accounts receivable ledger is posted daily and the general ledger is posted at the end of the month, the accounts receivable ledger total will equal the general ledger Accounts Receivable total only at the end of the month. Use an example to demonstrate the temporary "imbalance" that could exist during the month.

In-Class Exercise: Complete Problem ALT11-8A, ALT11-8B (15 minutes each)

❖ **Transparency Master 11-11 illustrates Figure 11-16 Accounting for Sales Returns and Allowances.**

❖ **PowerPoint Slides 11-62 through 11-65 present Sales Returns and Allowances.**

    D.   Sales returns and allowances (**See Figure 11-16**)
        1.   Require an entry in the general journal.
        2.   Posted daily
            a)   **In the accounts receivable ledger account:**
                (1)   Enter the date of the transaction in the Date column.
                (2)   Enter the amount of the debit or credit in the Debit or Credit column.
                (3)   Enter the new balance in the Balance column.
                (4)   Enter the journal page number from which each transaction is posted in the Posting Reference column.
            b)   **In the journal:**
                (1)   Enter a slash (/) followed by a check mark (✓) in the Posting Reference column of the journal for each transaction that is posted.

Teaching Tip

➢ Walk through the posting of a sales returns and allowances transaction to be sure students understand the dual posting of the credit to accounts receivable.

In-Class Exercise: Complete Exercise ALT11-5A, ALT11-5B (5 minutes each)

LO4

❖ Transparency Master 11-12 illustrates **Figure 11-17 Northern Micro Cash Receipts Journal (left and right sides)**

❖ PowerPoint Slides 11-66 through 11-113 present **credit card receipts and the Cash Receipts Journal**

IV. **Cash Receipts Journal (See Figure 11-17 and Figure 11-18)**
    A.   Special journal used to record only cash receipts.
        1.   Record cash receipts by entering the following information:
            a)   Date
            b)   Account credited (identify customer for any payment received)
            c)   Dollar amounts
        2.   Transactions include collections from customers, cash sales, bank credit card sales, receipt of revenue, and loans from bank.

Teaching Tips

➤ The last transaction illustrated involves signing a note to borrow money from the bank. If students ask what a note is, tell them this is simply a formal promise to repay the loan. The topic is covered fully in Chapter 18.

➤ As with the sales transactions, actually enter several cash receipt transactions in a general journal and cash receipts journal in class and compare the time required.

➤ Emphasize that cash sales are recorded in the cash receipts journal, not the sales journal. Students often think that all sales are recorded in the sales journal.

❖ Transparency Master 11-13 illustrates **Figure 11-19 Posting the Cash Receipts Journal to the General Ledger**

    B.   Posting from the cash receipts journal (**See Figure 11-19**)
        1.   **In the ledger account, daily:**
            a)   Enter the date of the transaction in the Date column
            b)   Enter the amount of the debit or credit in the Debit or Credit column.
            c)   Enter the new balance in the Balance columns under Debit or Credit.
            d)   Enter a CR and the journal page number in the Posting Reference Column.
        2.   **In the cash receipts journal, daily:**
            a)   Enter the ledger account number in the Posting Reference column for each account that is posted.
        3.   **In the cash receipts journal, monthly:**
            a)   Total the amount columns, verify that the total of the debit columns equals the total of the credit columns, and rule the columns.
        4.   **In the ledger account, monthly:**
            a)   Enter the date in the Date column.
            b)   Enter the amount of the debit or credit in the Debit or Credit column.

      c)   Enter the new balance in the Balance columns under Debit or Credit.

      d)   Enter a CR and the journal page number in the Posting Reference column.

5.   **In the cash receipts journal, monthly:**

      a)   Enter the ledger account number immediately below the column totals for each account that is posted.

      b)   Enter a check mark (✓) in the Posting Reference column for the cash sales and bank credit card sales, and immediately below the General Credit column.

In-Class Exercise: Complete Exercise ALT11-6A, ALT11-6B (15 minutes each)

❖   **Transparency Master 11-14 illustrates Figure 11-20 Posting the Cash Receipts Journal to the Accounts Receivable Ledger**

C.   Posting to the Accounts Receivable ledger **(See Figure 11-20)**

1.   **In the accounts receivable ledger account, daily:**

      a)   Enter the date of the transaction in the Date column

      b)   Enter the amount of the debit or credit in the Debit or Credit column.

      c)   Enter the new balance in the Balance column.

      d)   Enter a CR and the journal page number in the Posting Reference column.

2.   **In the cash receipts journal, daily:**

      a)   Enter a check mark (✓) in the Posting Reference column of the journal for each transaction that is posted.

Teaching Tip

➢   Have students explain every posting reference in the cash receipts journal, including when the posting was made and to what account. This will help you determine whether they understand the posting process.

LO5

❖   **PowerPoint Slides 11-114 through 11-116 present Schedule of Accounts Receivable**

V.   **Schedule of Accounts Receivable (See Figure 11-22)**

A.   Prepared to verify the sum of the accounts receivable ledger equals the controlling accounts receivable account balance.

Teaching Tip

➢   Have students compare the balances in the customer accounts in the accounts receivable subsidiary ledger with the amounts in the schedule of accounts receivable.

❖   **Transparency Master 11-15 illustrates Figure 11-21 General Ledger and Accounts Receivable Ledger after Posting.**

B.   List of all customers with an account balance at the end of the month **(See Figure 11-21).**

C. If the schedule does not agree with the accounts receivable balance, the error must be found.
   1. Verify the total of the schedule.
   2. Verify the postings to the accounts receivable ledger.
   3. Verify the totals in the sales and cash receipts journal.
   4. Verify the posting to Accounts Receivable in the general ledger.

In-Class Exercise: Complete Exercise ALT11-7A, ALT11-7B (10 minutes each)
In-Class Exercise: Complete Problem ALT11-11A, ALT11-11B (10 minutes each)

Learning Activity

1. Have your students visit a wholesale business and a retail business and have them ask the accounting or bookkeeping department how they handle sales, both cash and credit, and then relate what they learned to this chapter.

2. With their books closed, have the students write in detail 2 transactions that would be recorded in a sales journal, 3 transactions that would be recorded in a cash receipts journal, and 1 transaction that would be recorded in a general journal.

Critical Thinking Activity

Ask students: When does a sale become a sale? Nine times out of ten, the students will say a sale is a sale when the merchant receives the cash. They say this because they are so attuned to the cash basis of accounting. A sale is recorded when the merchandise changes hands. There is a transfer of title and ownership.

Homework Suggestions

LO1 Chapter 11 Study Guide Review Questions 1 through 8; Chapter 11 Study Guide Exercises 1, 2; End of Chapter Questions 1, 2

LO2 Chapter 11 Study Guide Review Questions 9 through 14; Chapter 13 Study Guide Review Questions 1, 2; End of Chapter Question 3; Exercise ALT11-2A, ALT11-2B

LO3 Chapter 11 Study Guide Review Questions 15 through 18; Chapter 13 Study Guide Review Questions 3 through 6; Chapter 11 Study Guide Exercise 3; Chapter 13 Study Guide Exercise 2; Chapter 13 Study Guide Problem 7; End of Chapter Questions 4, 5, 6, 7; Exercise ALT11-4A, ALT11-4B; Problem ALT11-2A, ALT11-2B

LO4 Chapter 13 Study Guide Review Questions 7, 8, 9; Chapter 13 Study Guide Exercise 3; Chapter 13 Study Guide Problems 6, 8; End of Chapter Questions 8, 9, 10; Problems ALT11-9A, ALT11-9B, ALT11-10A, ALT11-10B

LO5 **Chapter 11** Study Guide Review Questions 19, 20; Chapter 11 Study Guide Problem 7; End of Chapter Question 11

Entire Chapter:
Mastery Problem and Challenge Problem.

1. How much more complex is accounting for a merchandise business—since it is in the middle of a chain?
2. So now revenue has three parts—sales, returns, and discounts?
3. Why do you keep track of discounts if you never receive that money?
4. Same thing with allowances—you never received the money?
5. With these cash discounts, what if the seller offers 2/eom, n/60 and you buy on the 28th of the month—do you get only two or three days?
6. How often do we have to post sales on account?
7. Do all credit card companies charge the same fee to the retailer?
8. Do some businesses keep track of cash sales customers?
9. In a schedule of accounts receivable, do you list customers with a zero balance?
10. Since only credit sales go in the sales journal, will a large retail store have one?

Learning Objectives

LO1 Define merchandise purchases transactions.
LO2 Describe and use merchandise purchases accounts and compute gross profit.
LO3 Describe and use the purchases journal and accounts payable ledger.
LO4 Describe and use the cash payments journal and accounts payable ledger.
LO5 Prepare a schedule of accounts payable.

LO1

❖ **Transparency Master 12-1 illustrates Figure 12-1 Purchasing Process Documents**

❖ **PowerPoint Slides 12-1 through 12-12 present Merchandise Purchase Transactions**

I. Merchandise Purchase Transactions **(See Figure 12-1)**
    A. **Purchases**
        1. Refers to merchandise acquired for sale in a retail business.
        2. Procedures for purchasing and documentation vary, depending on the nature and size of the business.

Teaching Tips

➢ Purchasing procedures vary greatly across businesses. Have students describe the purchasing process where they work, and discuss differences identified.

➢ Walk through Figure 12-1 and explain the role each document plays in the purchasing process. Students often confuse the purposes of the purchase requisition and purchase order.

❖ **Transparency Master 12-2 illustrates Figure 12-2 Purchase Requisition.**

    B. **Purchase requisition (See Figure 12-2)**
        1. Form used to request the purchase of assets.
        2. Authorized person prepares and sends form to the purchasing department.
        3. Copies are sent to
            a) Purchasing department
            b) Accounting department
            c) Kept by the department that prepared the requisition

Teaching Tip

➢ Explain that comparing the purchase invoice with the purchase requisition, purchase order, and receiving report is an example of good internal control. This procedure helps ensure that the business pays only for the goods it ordered and received, and at the correct price. Also emphasize the importance of the purchase invoice as a <u>source document</u> used to record purchase transactions.

❖ **Transparency Master 12-3 illustrates Figure 12-3 Purchase Order**

    C.   **Purchase order (See Figure 12-3)**
        1.   Written order to buy goods from a specific vendor.
        2.   Copies are sent to
           a)   Vendor to order the goods
           b)   Accounting department
           c)   Purchasing department
           d)   Originator of the purchase requisition
           e)   Receiving area

❖ **Transparency Master 12-4 illustrates Figure 12-4 Purchase Invoice**

    D.   Receiving report and the **purchase invoice (See Figure 12-4)**
        1.   **Receiving report** is prepared when goods are received.
        2.   **Invoice** is prepared by the seller and shipped to the buyer.
           a)   Accounting department compares the purchase invoice with the purchase requisition, purchase order, and receiving report.
           b)   Invoice is paid if everything is correct.

❖ **Transparency Master 12-5 illustrates Figure 12-5 Purchase Invoice with Trade Discount**

    E.   Cash and trade discounts **(See Figure 12-5)**
        1.   Cash discounts are available if the bill is paid within the discount period.
        2.   **Trade discounts** are percentage reductions from the total amount of the invoice.

Teaching Tip

➢   Explain the difference between cash and trade discounts. Cash discounts are given because a bill is paid promptly. Trade discounts are given because of the position of a business in the marketing chain. For example, a manufacturer will give a trade discount to a wholesaler because of the role the wholesaler plays in distributing the products to retailers. Emphasize that trade discount amounts are not entered into either the seller's or the buyer's accounts.

In-Class Exercise: Complete Exercise ALT12-1A, ALT12-1B (5 minutes each)
In-Class Exercise: Complete Exercise ALT12-2A, ALT12-2B (10 minutes each)

LO2

❖ **Transparency Master 12-6 illustrates Figure 12-6 Accounting for Merchandise Purchases Transactions**

❖ **PowerPoint Slides 12-13 through 12-58 present Merchandise Purchase Accounts and Computation of Gross Profit**

II. Merchandise Purchases Accounts **(See Figure 12-6)**
   A. Purchases account
      1. Used to record the cost of merchandise purchased.
      2. Amount of each purchase is debited to the account.
   B. Purchases returns and allowances
      1. Contra-purchases account used to record purchases returns and allowances.
      2. Reported as a deduction from Purchases on the income statement.
      3. Amount of each purchase returned or allowance granted is credited to the account.

Teaching Tip

➢ Caution students that Purchases Returns and Allowances is used to record only <u>merchandise</u> returns and allowances. If an asset other than merchandise is returned, that specific asset account is credited.

   C. Purchases discounts account
      1. Used to record cash discounts on purchases.
      2. Reported as a deduction from Purchases on the income statement.
      3. Cash discounts on purchases are credited to the account.

Teaching Tips

➢ Point out that returns, allowances, and cash discounts are credited to separate accounts rather than directly to Purchases so that the business can keep track of these activities.

➢ Purchases discounts can be recorded using the <u>gross method</u> or the <u>net method</u>. The gross method is described in this chapter. The net method is described in the Appendix.

   D. Freight-in account
      1. Used to report transportation charges on merchandise purchased.
      2. **FOB shipping point** means the transportation charges are paid by the buyer and are debited to the account.
      3. **FOB destination** means that transportation charges are paid by the seller and the freight-in account is not used.

Teaching Tips

➢ Students are accustomed to seeing advertising of products at a price "plus shipping and handling." Ask students what FOB terms are implied by such ads.

➢ Point out that the two shipping methods do not change the cost of the goods being purchased. FOB shipping point results in the purchase price of the goods and the shipping charges being separately identified on the books of the purchases. FOB destination does not result in separate identification. However, the seller of the goods includes the shipping charges in the cost of the items being purchased.

    E.   Computation of **gross profit** (also called **gross margin**) **(See Figure 12-7)**
        1.   Net sales minus cost of goods sold equals gross profit.
        2.   Merchandise available minus ending inventory equals **cost of goods sold** (also called **cost of merchandise sold**).
        3.   Gross profit tells management the amount of sales revenue that are left to cover operation expenses.
        4.   Computing gross profit
            a)   Compute net sales
            b)   Compute goods available for sale
            c)   Compute cost of goods sold
            d)   Compute gross profit

Teaching Tip

➢   Have students play the role of management. Assume that gross profit has shrunk because of competition. What expenses can be reduced to keep the business profitable? See if students are willing to eliminate jobs. This can provide a valuable real-world lesson.

In-Class Exercise: Complete Exercise ALT12-4A, ALT12-4B (10 minutes each)

LO3

❖   Transparency Master 12-8 illustrates Figure 12-8 Purchases Entered in General Journal

❖   Transparency Master 12-9 illustrates Figure 12-9 Northern Micro Purchases Journal

❖   Transparency Master 12-10 illustrates Figure 12-10 Purchases Journal with Freight-In Column

❖   PowerPoint Slides 12-59 through 12-66 present the Purchases Journal

III.   **Purchases Journal (See Figure 12-8, Figure 12-9 and Figure 12-10)**
    A.   Special journal used to record only purchases of merchandise on account.
        1.   Each recording consists of
            a)   Date
            b)   Invoice number
            c)   Supplier (from whom purchased)
            d)   Dollar amount

Teaching Tips

➢   Emphasize that the purchases journal illustrated here is used to record only merchandise purchased on account. Purchases of supplies, equipment, etc. must be recorded elsewhere. You might want to point out that there is another type of purchases journal, often called an acquisitions journal, which can be used to record all types of purchases on account.

➢   Actually enter the five transactions on text page 57 in a general journal and in a purchases journal in class and compare the time required.

In-Class Exercise: Complete Exercise ALT12-5A, ALT12-5B (10 minutes each)

❖ **Transparency Master 12-11 illustrates Figure 12-11 Posting the Purchases Journal to the General Ledger**

    B.   Posting the Purchases Journal **(See Figure 12-11)**
        1.   **In the purchases journal, monthly:**
            a)   Total and rule the amount column.
        2.   **In the ledger account, monthly:**
            a)   Enter the date in the Date column.
            b)   Enter the amount of the debit or credit in the Debit or Credit column.
            c)   Enter the new balance in the Balance columns under Debit or Credit.
            d)   Enter a P and the journal page number in the Posting Reference column.
        3.   **In the purchases journal, monthly:**
            a)   Enter the Purchase and Accounts Payable account numbers immediately below the column total.

Teaching Tip

➢   Have students compare the purchases journal posting process in Figure 12-12 with the sales journal posting process in Figure 11-15. Seeing the similarity of the two systems can help students understand both of them.

❖ **Transparency Master 12-12 illustrates Figure 12-12 Posting the Purchases Journal to the Accounts Payable Ledger**

    C.   Posting to the Subsidiary Accounts Payable Ledger **(See Figure 12-12)**
        1.   Separate ledger containing an individual accounts payable for each supplier
        2.   Controlling accounts payable account is maintained in the general ledger
        3.   Posted daily so the supplier information is current
        4.   **In the accounts payable ledger account, daily:**
            a)   Enter the date of the transaction in the Date column.
            b)   Enter the amount of the debit or credit in the Debit or Credit Column.
            c)   Enter the new balance in the Balance column.
            d)   Enter a P and the journal page number in the Posting Reference column.
        5.   **In the purchases journal, daily:**
            a)   Enter a check mark (✓) in the Posting Reference column of the journal for each transaction that is posted.

Teaching Tip

➢   Note that, if the accounts payable ledger is posted daily and the general ledger is posted at the end of the month, the accounts payable ledger total will equal the general ledger Accounts Payable total only at the end of the month. Use an example to demonstrate the temporary "imbalance" that could exist during the month.

In-Class Exercise: Complete Exercise ALT12-5A, ALT12-5B (15 minutes each)

❖ **Transparency Master 12-13 illustrates Figure 12-13 Accounting for Purchases Returns and Allowances**

❖ **PowerPoint Slides 12-67 through 12-69 present purchase returns and allowances**

      D.   Purchase returns and allowances **(See Figure 12-13)**
          1.   General journal entry is required.
          2.   Postings are made daily.
              a)   **In the accounts payable ledger account:**
                 (1)   Enter the date of the transaction in the Date column.
                 (2)   Enter the amount of the debit or credit in the Debit or Credit column
                 (3)   Enter the new balance in the Balance column
                 (4)   Enter the journal page number from which each transaction is posted in the Posting Reference column
              b)   **In the journal:**
                 (1)   Enter a slash (/) followed by a check mark (✓) in the Posting Reference column of the journal for each transaction that is posted

Teaching Tip

➢   Walk through the posting of a purchases returns and allowances transaction to be sure students understand the dual posting of the debit to accounts payable.

LO4

❖ **Transparency Master 12-14 illustrates Figure 12-14 Northern Micro Cash Payments Journal (left and right sides)**

❖ **PowerPoint Slides 12-70 through 12-93 present the Cash Payments Journal**

IV.   **Cash Payments Journal (See Figure 12-14)**
      A.   Types of cash payments
          1.   Payment of expense
          2.   Cash purchase
          3.   Payment of accounts payable
          4.   Payment of notes payable
          5.   Withdrawal by an owner
      B.   Cash payments are recorded with
          1.   Date
          2.   Check number
          3.   Account debited
          4.   Dollar amounts

Teaching Tip

➢   Emphasize that cash purchases are recorded in the cash payments journal, not in the purchases journal.

In-Class Exercise: Complete Exercise ALT12-7A, ALT12-7B (15 minutes each)

❖ **Transparency Master 12-15 illustrates Figure 12-15 Posting the Cash Payments Journal to the General Ledger.**

    C.   Posting the cash payments journal **(See Figure 12-15)**
        1.   **In the ledger account, daily:**
            a)   Enter the date of the transaction in the Date column.
            b)   Enter the amount of the debit or credit in the Debit or Credit column.
            c)   Enter the new balance in the Balance columns under Debit or Credit.
            d)   Enter a CP and the journal page number in the Posting Reference column.
        2.   **In the cash payments journal, daily:**
            a)   Enter the ledger account number in the Posting Reference column for each account that is posted.
        3.   **In the cash payments journal, monthly:**
            a)   Total the amount columns, verify that the total of the debit columns equals the total of the credit columns, and rule the columns.
        4.   **In the ledger account, monthly:**
            a)   Enter the date in the Date column.
            b)   Enter the amount of the debit or credit in the Debit or Credit column.
            c)   Enter the new balance in the Balance columns under Debit or Credit.
            d)   Enter a CP and the journal page number in the Posting Reference column.
        5.   **In the cash payments journal, monthly:**
            a)   Enter the ledger account number immediately below the column totals for each account that is posted.
            b)   Enter a check mark (✓) in the Posting Reference column for the cash purchases, and immediately below the General Debit column.

❖ **Transparency Master 12-16 illustrates Figure 12-16 Posting the Cash Payments Journal to the Accounts Payable Ledger**

    D.   Posting to the Accounts Payable ledger **(See Figure 12-16)**
        1.   **In the accounts payable ledger account, daily:**
            a)   Enter the date of the transaction in the Date column.
            b)   Enter the amount of the debit or credit in the Debit or Credit column.
            c)   Enter the new balance in the Balance column.
            d)   Enter a CP and the journal page number in the Posting Reference column.
        2.   **In the cash payments journal, daily:**
            a)   Enter a check mark (✓) in the Posting Reference column of the journal for each transaction that is posted.

Teaching Tip

➢   Have students explain every posting reference in the cash payments journal, including when the posting was made and to what account. This will help you determine whether they understand the posting process.

LO5

❖ **Transparency Master 12-17 illustrates Figure 12-17 General Ledger and Accounts Payable Ledger after Posting**

❖ **PowerPoint Slides 12-94 through 12-96 present Schedule of Accounts Payable**

V. **Schedule of Accounts Payable (See Figure 12-17 and Figure 12-18)**
   A. Prepared to verify that the sum of the accounts payable ledger balances equals the Accounts Payable balance.

Teaching Tip

➢ Have students compare the balances in the supplier accounts in the accounts payable subsidiary ledger with the amounts listed in the schedule of accounts payable.

   B. Errors must be located and corrected.
      1. Verify the total of the schedule.
      2. Verity the posting to the accounts payable ledger.
      3. Verify the totals in the purchases and cash payments journals.
      4. Verity the posting to Accounts Payable in the general ledger.

In-Class Exercise: Complete Exercise ALT12-8A, ALT12-8B (5 minutes each)
In-Class Exercise: Complete Problem ALT12-13A, ALT12-13B (10 minutes each)

Learning Activities

1. Have your students visit one or more of their favorite retail stores and have them ask the bookkeeping department how and when the store's purchases are made and how and when their payments are made and then relate their findings to this chapter.

2. With their books closed, have the students write in detail 2 transactions that would be recorded in a purchases journal, 3 transactions that would be recorded in a cash payments journal, and 1 transaction that would be recorded in a general journal.

Critical Thinking Activity

It may seem to students that a lot of paperwork is generated to purchase goods. Have students discuss the reasons for preparing purchase requisitions, purchase orders, receiving reports, and purchase invoices. Part of the discussion should center on the problems that could result by not preparing each type of paperwork. If necessary, point out that the reports prepared and received by the buyer act as checks and balances in the purchasing procedure. These chains of authorization are used to prevent the unauthorized purchase of goods and other property. These reports also act as source documents for the data entered in the company's accounting systems.

LO1   Chapter 12 Study Guide Review Questions 1 through 7; Chapter 12 Study Guide Exercises 1, 2, 3, 4, 5; End of Chapter Questions 1, 2.

LO2   Chapter 12 Study Guide Review Questions 8 through 12; Chapter 12 Study Guide Exercise 6; End of Chapter Questions 3, 4; Exercise ALT12-3A, ALT12-3B.

LO3   Chapter 12 Study Guide Review Questions 13 through 17; Chapter 13 Study Guide Review Questions 10 through 14; Chapter 13 Study Guide Exercise 4; Chapter 13 Study Guide Problem 9; End of Chapter Questions 5, 6, 7, 8; Exercise ALT12-5A, ALT12-5B, ALT12-6A, ALT12-6B; Problems ALT12-9A, ALT12-9B, ALT12-10A, ALT12-10B.

LO4   Chapter 13 Study Guide Review Questions 15 through 18; Chapter 13 Study Guide Exercise 5; Chapter 13 Study Guide Problem 10; End of Chapter Questions 9, 10, 11; Problems ALT12-11A, ALT12-11B, ALT12-2A, ALT12-12B.

LO5   Chapter 12 Study Guide Review Question 18; Chapter 12 Study Guide Problem 10; Chapter 13 Study Guide Exercise 1; End of Chapter Question 12

Entire Chapter:
Mastery Problem and Challenge Problem.

1. Are purchases sort of treated like expenses?
2. Do all retail or merchandise businesses use all of these journals?
3. So, the invoice comes from our supplier to us, the retailer?
4. If we pay in time, why do we keep track of the discounts?
5. Do we have an account for trade discounts?
6. How often do we have to post purchases on account?
7. Is freight-in an expense account or something else?
8. Why, if we don't pay for it, do we account for an allowance on a purchase?
9. In the schedule of accounts payable, do you list all of your suppliers or just the ones you owe?
10. Are purchases of office supplies or cleaning supplies entered into the purchases journal?

Learning Objectives

LO1 Describe the net-price method of recording purchases.
LO2 Record purchases and cash payments using the net-price method.

LO1

❖   **PowerPoint Slides 12Apx-1 and 12Apx-2 present Recording Purchases Methods**

I.   Net-Price Method
    A.   Alternative approach to Gross-Price method of accounting for purchases.
    B.   Purchases are recorded at the net amount, assuming that all available cash discounts will be taken.

LO2

❖   **PowerPoint Slides 12Apx-3 through 12Apx-12 present Comparison of Gross-Price and Net-Price Methods**

II.   Compare **Gross-Price Method** and **Net-Price Method**
    A.   Purchase merchandise for $100 on account with credit terms of 2/10, n/30
       1.   Gross-Price Method
          a)   Debit Purchases $100
          b)   Credit Accounts Payable $100
       2.   Net-Price Method
          a)   Debit Purchases $98 ($100 - $2) ($100 $\times$ 2% = $2 discount)
          b)   Credit Accounts Payable $98

III.   Payment made within discount period
    A.   Gross-Price Method
       1.   Debit Accounts Payable $100
       2.   Credit Cash $98
       3.   Credit Purchases Discount $2
    B.   Net-Price Method
       1.   Debit Accounts Payable $98
       2.   Credit Cash $98

IV.   Payment made after discount period expires
    A.   Gross-Price Method
       1.   Debit Accounts Payable $100
       2.   Credit Cash $100
    B.   Net-Price Method
       1.   Debit Accounts Payable $98

2.   Debit Purchases Discounts Lost $2
        a)   temporary owner's equity account
        b)   normal debit balance
3.   Credit Cash $100

In-Class Exercise: Complete Exercise 12Apx-1A (15 minutes)

Homework Suggestions

LO2 Chapter 12 Study Guide Apx. Exercise, End of Appendix Exercise 12Apx-1B